A Gift from GOD

by Jerry Bishop

Copyright © 2012 by Jerry Bishop
First Edition – June 2012

ISBN
978-1-77097-608-5 (Hardcover)
978-1-77097-609-2 (Paperback)
978-1-77097-610-8 (eBook)

All rights reserved.

No part of this publication may be reproduced in any form, or by any means, electronic or mechanical, including photocopying, recording, or any information browsing, storage, or retrieval system, without permission in writing from the publisher.

Published by:

FriesenPress
Suite 300 – 852 Fort Street
Victoria, BC, Canada V8W 1H8

www.friesenpress.com

Distributed to the trade by The Ingram Book Company

Table Of Contents

Dedication v
Acknowledgments vi
Prologue 1
"Boy Meets Girl" 3
"A Hawaiian Wedding" 13
"Back To Being A Civilian" 28
"Starting A "New" Life" 41
"Back Home Again" 48
"Joann's Story" 62
"The Investigation" 75
"A Spared Life" 86
"The Fatal Call" 91
"A New Chapter Of Our Lives" 104
"A Miracle Called Andrea" 113
"God's Mysterious Ways" 121
"Life As It Stands" 125
Epilogue 134
PaPa's Favorite Photos 138

Dedication

I wish to dedicate this book to my granddaughter Andrea that inspired and gave me the reasons for writing it. As you read this, you will understand why she has had such an impact on my life as well as my family and all those she touches on a daily basis.

Andrea's big smile . . . .

ACKNOWLEDGMENTS

Being the spontaneous type person I am, one night while watching TV, I decided to write a book that I felt could possibly save thousands of "unborn children" from the abortionist's knife. You can imagine the disarray this placed on my home. Here I am, 72 years of age, working a full-time job selling food and now I have decided to sit in front of a computer using every spare minute I have in the evenings and weekends, to write a book.

So now it is time for me to acknowledge those people who were very supportive and such a big help to me.

My Mother, "Grandma K." 94 years of age, who lives with us, does all of the cooking and baking in our household. She is also a great help in many other ways.

My biggest thank you goes to my wife of almost 52 years. In the beginning, she did not want to relive our life, line by line. Later on, there was many a night when I saw her sitting at the computer, with tears rolling down her cheeks. It was a very trying experience for her but I would not give up the idea of writing: "Our story." I felt that it was that important to share it with as many people as possible.

At some point we involved her sister Michele from Canada. This seemed to make a difference for Nickie and I began to see a level of interest that was not there before. Together, they started checking my spelling and layouts and made corrections that I usually agreed with. It's almost funny when I think about this; when I met Nickie in 1959 she probably had a vocabulary of some 50 English words and now she and her sister, both French speaking, are doing the editing of my book, before publishing.

There is someone else I want to give a big thank you too also: Michele's husband Serge, who gave up a lot of time with his wife, while she worked on the computer till all hours of the night.

Last but not least, I would like to thank my LORD for giving me the inspiration and knowledge to put my thoughts onto paper for others to hopefully enjoy and in some way be able to relate to.

PROLOGUE

It is Saturday morning, January 21st, 2012. As of last night, the writing of my book came to a conclusion. My sister-in-law Michele, who has worked with my wife Nicole, hours on end doing editing and layout work, asked me: "What about the prologue, what was it that motivated you to write this book, which is basically biographical, at your age?"

I think my initial response came as a shock to her. MONEY was my primary motivation for doing this. For years I have watched TV personalities, present and former politicians, being given an opportunity to introduce books they have written, by appearing on national television, which generally earns them a small fortune.

I've read many of these books and found some to be entertaining and some to be informational. So I thought to myself: I have a story to tell that may save thousands of unborn children's lives. Why not write it?

In doing some of my research, I found that the money idea was starting to take a back seat into my reasons for writing the book. One article I read was about how medical technology has reached a point whereby it is now possible to determine, two to three months after conception that the unborn child a mother is carrying, is to be born with Down Syndrome. Not only is the mother encouraged to have an abortion but the statistics are that 95% of them do and consequently are depriving themselves and their family of one of the greatest joy they could possibly have in life.

This of course hit home because 6½ years ago, we were given custody of a child with DS and we know the joy she has brought to our lives. I decided to write this book as a biography of some 50+ years of my life. In doing so, I basically relived these years and began to understand what effect my belief in God has had on my life and how He has always been there for me. It also helped me realize God's plan for me and why my life was spared on three different occasions.

It also became obvious to me that God has blessed me in so many ways, starting with the great faith that my wife has always had, which often carried us thru some really rough periods in the 52 years we've been married.

There is definitely a rainbow after a storm, if you just look for it!

CHAPTER ONE
"BOY MEETS GIRL"

For months I have been saying that I wanted to write a book about a little girl named "ANDREA".

So, I asked myself, where do I begin? You see, I have never written anything before and I am really not sure I can put my innermost feelings onto paper, for others to read and hopefully enjoy.

Therefore, I will start by telling you a little bit about the two persons who made this book a reality. My name is Jerry; my wife of some 52 years is Nicole or "Nickie" as most friends call her. Yes, we are both in our 70's and yes, we still love each other very much. When most people ask: "How did you two meet, two people from two separate countries, speaking different languages?" My reply is usually followed with: "You've got to be kidding, right?" No kidding, it's all TRUE. You see, Nickie was a French speaking Canadian who was visiting our country while her parents attended a chiropractic college, in Indianapolis, In. and I, a mid-westerner from a small town in Indiana, was home on leave from the U.S. Navy for 30 days.

In the fall of 1959 I had been attending a USN Radio School in San Diego, California. Upon completion, I was granted a 30 day leave in order to come home, visit my family and friends before being assigned to the fleet and making my first trip to Japan, over the Christmas holidays.

The trip home from San Diego, seemed a little longer this time for some reason. Probably had something to do with the fact that for the previous 6 months, I had been in Radio school listening to "dits" and "dahs" for the better part of 8 hours per day. Not only was my brain tired, my back was killing me too. What I really needed was a few hours sleep in a nice firm bed, when I got home.

When I arrived, I called my girlfriend to tell her I needed to catch a few hours of sleep and I would see her the following evening. Not a good idea for sure. She became quite upset that I didn't want to come see her and seemed to really want to make an issue about it. Was this the same girl I had grown to love and hoped to marry and build a life with? Something was certainly different. What, I didn't know, but different for sure. I guess I could have asked her point blank: "Is there someone else"? Maybe I feared the answer, so I suggested we not see each other for a few days and give ourselves time to decide, if there was to be a future for us.

By the middle of the following week, I had decided to accept what had happened. I then went to see her for the last time. We both realized that this union was not to be. We parted with a hug and a tear, knowing we were doing what was the right thing for our futures.

To put a conclusion to this part of the story, let me share with you what happened some 20 years later. One night while on a road trip to Evansville, In. as a traveling salesman, I decided to try and make things right between two persons that at one time had meant so much to each other. I called her mother and she gave me a phone number for Nancy in the state of Washington where she was presently living. The only thing she asked of me was to be nice to her daughter. I assured her that we had both grown up and it would be a good call, for us both.

The phone call was kind of short but meaningful for us both, I believe. She had married a service man, who was killed in action and was the mother of two fine sons. I shared with her my condolences. Nancy was basically a good person and she didn't need this sadness in her life.

I then told her about my family too. It seemed we had both been blessed with children and were getting along in life, as best we could. She was teaching nursing and I was selling little metal fasteners for conveyor belts.

I said I had always regretted any hurt I had caused that night in 1959 and her response was, it wasn't hurt, as much as it was anger. She accepted my apology and we continued talking about our respective families, for a few more minutes. We never spoke again. A few years later, I read that she had died of breast cancer. I'm so glad we had had our talk before her life ended here on earth.

What happened next will probably cause you to say: "You've got to be kidding, right"?

Jerry's mother, Grandma K.

My mother, who we will call **Grandma K**, suggested that I go visit with Ruth and Warren W. They had a daughter about my age and maybe she had a friend that I could chum around with for the balance of my leave.

It was good seeing them. We used to be neighbors and while I was growing up, Ruth had sort of watched over me after school, until my mother returned from work each day.

I told them of my dilemma and Ruth says to Mary Ann, their daughter: "How about that nice French speaking girl you worked with at New York Life Insurance Co. I think Jerry would like her."

Next thing I knew, they had given me a phone number and I am talking with her about a luncheon date for the next day. Of course, she wondered who I was and how I had obtained her phone number. At first Mary Ann had told me to say I was a fellow that I had gone to school with. He was a Mama's boy and Nickie had a couple dates with him. I really did not care for him and I found out later that she didn't either. Thinking I was he, she turned down every request for a date that I made. Tied up for 6 months, she said, then that loud laugh again. Mary Ann always had a crackling laugh that was almost totally uncontrollable so, she gave it away as to who I was and all. She knew who had put me up to this. We agreed to meet the next day at 12:00 noon for lunch.

What happened next was not normal for me. As a rule, I am always early but this time, I got in traffic and was late for our date. When I arrived, she had left. She had told the switchboard operator that she had better things to do then miss lunch because of someone who obviously couldn't tell time. WOW I said under my breath,

I am finally going to meet an independent girl. Most of the girls that I had dated were sort of hanger-on criers and this was something I really didn't care for. I watched a lot of movies when younger and I had always enjoyed and respected the women that played the stronger parts, for some reason. I was anxious to meet Nickie, if for no other reason than she sounded like a strong person that I would like.

The switchboard operator said "you may as well sit down" after she determined that we had never met before and that I would have had a problem picking her out of a crowd, at the local lunch counter down the street.

The next 45 minutes I waited, seemed like forever. Then all of a sudden a lady in a black wool dress that hugged every inch of her body, walked through the door. I almost fell off the couch. My first thought was: had I died and went to heaven or what? She was without a doubt the most beautiful person I had ever laid my eyes on. Even Ruth Roman, my favorite actress, couldn't hold a candle to her beauty.

Nickie before marriage

I had secretly been in love with Ruth Roman, an actress from the fifty's era, most of my young life and all of a sudden, here she was, standing right in front of me. Hand extended to introduce herself. I was so excited, I believe I extended the wrong hand and started to stutter a bit. With a little help from the good Lord, I was able to contain myself and get a phone number, so I could call her later in the day, after I had time to calm down a bit.

That afternoon I had an appointment to get a haircut from an old Army buddy of my stepfather. His name was Jimmy, too. He asked me how I liked the Navy and what I would be doing while home on leave. I said I was not really sure. I had just this morning met a really nice girl and I would probably spend most of my time with her. We'll see what comes of it.

Later on that afternoon, I stopped by the house and my sister Martha was doing her bi-monthly cleaning to earn a little extra cash. Without going into all the details, I told Martha that I had met the most beautiful woman I had ever seen earlier today and if she would have me, I would spend the rest of my life with her.

I think Martha knew me better than most and her only comment was: "I hope to meet her soon." She did on Saturday evening. It was obvious to me that Martha and Bob, her husband, liked Nickie very much. We left around 11:00 P.M. for the drive home. Nickie sat next to me and we were holding hands, when she said: "My relatives told me I would probably never return to Canada. I would meet someone in the U.S., a *knight* dressed in *shinning armour* and be whisked away forever." I still find it hard to believe what I said in response: "I sure hope I turn out to be this *knight* they were talking about!" Dead SILENCE followed. I felt her squeeze my hand a little. We did not talk again, until I pulled up in front of her parent's apartment.

I had promised to attend mass with her in the morning so we didn't talk a lot and thinking about it now . . . what more could have been said anyway. I assured her that I would be on time and after we would go to meet one of the most important people in my young life, my Grandmother Jenkins, who lived in a small town near the Indiana state line, next to Illinois.

Need I say, I did not sleep very well that night! My emotions were all over the place. Was I going too fast, would I lose her? All I knew for sure was that I just wanted to put my arms around her and hold her close, so she could not get away. I had never experienced these feelings before, not with anyone. They were wonderful and scary at the same time. I think I fell asleep in the early dawn, to awake to a beautiful fall morning. The mass was nice but kind of confusing to me. My mother was a Methodist and my stepfather a Catholic, so we never attended a church of any kind on a regular basis.

When the service ended, we picked up my parents and off we went to Grandma's house. I understood later that Nickie's parents were a little upset with their daughter, going this far out of town, with a stranger. The only thing they had heard in Canada was that a sailor has a girl in every port. Now that we have a little girl who is 10 years old, I can understand the thoughts that must have been going through their minds. It was a good drive and when we arrived, there was still a lot of food preparation to be completed before the traditional Sunday dinner. Nickie pitched right in and told me she would see me later, when all was ready.

I went to the living room and started to watch a football game. All I can remember is that it was snowing at game site and the Baltimore COLTS were playing. I had obviously fallen asleep because the next thing I recall was a tap on my shoulder telling me that dinner was ready. As I swung around to put my shoes on, Nickie sat down beside me and said: "Did you mean what I thought you meant, last night?" I said, yes. I did. I then said: "Nickie there is something about me that you should know. I am a very spontaneous type person. I'm not afraid to tell you that I could fall in love with you and I probably already have. I know it is fast but I have never felt this way about anyone before, of this I am sure." She then stopped me and looked into my eyes and said: "Then YES, I will marry you and we will spend our lives together, until we are called to our next life. Now, let's go eat before the dinner gets cold."

Am I still sleeping, or did this just happen? Oh how I hope it is the latter.

I meet a girl on Thursday, asks her to marry me on Saturday and she says YES on Sunday. Now I'm sure you understand why people say . . . "You've got to be kidding, right"? And, we have been together for 52 years. I also realized at that time the reason why things did not work out between my former girlfriend and I: GOD had a better plan for my life.

Something else that is kind of important to share with you is the fact that we didn't enjoy the *honeymoon* until AFTER THE WEDDING. And as a matter of fact, Nickie said YES to me before we had our first KISS. So, the next time you hear your grandparents referring to the good ole days, listen real well to them. They know what they are talking about.

CHAPTER TWO
"A HAWAIIAN WEDDING"

I just said to my wife Nickie: "Well, I got through the first chapter and I am quite pleased with it." I must admit though, I have edited it 4 or 5 times to assure myself that it's what I really wanted to say. So what could I write or do that would be more exciting then how we met and fell in love with one another? Well, how about what happened next?

Keep in mind I have 2 more weeks before flying back to Pearl Harbor, in the Hawaiian Islands. During this time, Nickie continued going to work everyday, which gave me a lot of time to try and find a Catholic priest that would agree to marry us. This was not an easy task, as I was soon to discover. I even had one priest ask if she was pregnant. At some point in my telling him our story, I must have lost him somewhere. So, I moved on. I then met a very young and modern priest Father Rippenger, at the St. Joseph Cathedral, in Indianapolis. We agreed to meet that evening after supper to discuss our plans.

At 5:00 P.M., I picked Nickie up after a long day's work and we stopped at my favorite restaurant, Steak N' Shake for a hamburger and fries, before going to the church to meet with the father.

As best as I can recall, the meeting lasted maybe an hour or so. Father Rippenger was what you would call a progressive priest. He seemed to be open-minded about many things. Right before we left he said: "I don't know why I am going to do this but I see something in the two of you that tells me it is right that you should marry and have a family together. I will be pleased to preside over your wedding."

This is something I believe we both needed to hear. I knew Nickie's mother was against it and my own mother had never made a decision in her entire life without thinking about it for a few days first. It helped us to believe in our decision, which I felt we both needed at that time.

The next evening we went to pick out her engagement ring. It wasn't large nor was it expensive but what it meant to us was far more important. It was a commitment of our feelings for each other.

The more we talked and got to know each other, the more I realized that I had made the right choice. This was the person I wanted to be the mother of my children. She must have felt the same, because our love seemed to grow each day.

At some point during the following days, before I left to return to Pearl Harbor, it was decided that maybe we were going a little bit too fast.

So we decided that maybe a later date would be better for the wedding and family concerns, in general. I still had my trip to Japan when I arrived back in Pearl, and that was for 4 months. Maybe we should delay the wedding for spring time. We would write to each other about it and then decide.

Father Rippenger agreed with our decision and we never saw or talked to him again. Thru the years, I often thought of making contact with him. I think it would please him to know that his assessment of Nickie and I was correct back in 1959.

Point of interest: Well, I finally did it! I found out that he lives near Tampa, Florida and when I talked with him, we agreed to meet soon. Needless to say, he was very surprised to hear from me and to find out that Nickie and I were still married.

During my final week of leave, Nickie and I spent every waken moment together. We had a lot to talk about and a lot to learn about each other. I hate to admit it but I knew almost nothing about Canada. Cold temperatures and POLAR BEARS was the sum total of my knowledge. Well, the bears are in Alaska and it is cold in Montreal. So, I was half right anyway. We laughed a lot and became good friends by week's end.

I promised to write and write often. I actually wrote my first letter on the plane ride to Los Angeles, CA, a gas stop before the 2400 mile flight to Honolulu, Hawaii, the home of Pearl Harbor. I wonder now, what could I have possibly written. My wife and I are now having problems remembering some of what took place some 50 years ago. She says it is not always important anyway. Being a detailed type person, as I am, we will agree to disagree on this, as I am the one that is really writing the book anyway. She helps me to remember different things that are important to her, which should be included in the book. That's what teamwork is all about, right?

After Radio school was completed, I had been assigned to the U.S.S. Lipan, ATF-85. She was an ocean going tug boat scheduled for a 4 month tour of duty with the first stop being, Yokuska, Japan in early January 1960.

U.S.S. Grapple ARS-7

When I got back from leave, I met with the executive officer of the Lipan and requested a transfer of assignment to a ship that would be returning to Pearl, that same month. To my amazement, he looked at a ledger and told me the **U.S.S. Grapple ARS-7**, was to leave Yokuska on the same day we were to arrive. She was heading home after a 4-month tour also. He would do whatever, to see that I was on the returning vessel.

He then congratulated me on my upcoming marriage. He also reminded me that by being a radioman, I would be the first to know if the transfer was approved. We would receive a radio message from the Seventh Fleet Headquarters to advise, YES or NO. You can imagine, when the Lipan and I left Pearl for our trip to Japan, I was glued to the radio room's incoming files, for the message to arrive. 3 days before arriving in Yokuska, the message came in: *Transfer request approved for J.B. Bishop, RM3, S/N classified. To take place upon Lipan's ATF-85 arrival and Grapple's ARS-7 departure from Yokuska, Japan harbor.* Was I blessed or what?

Being a Radioman, I was on the bridge as we pulled in the harbor. With my looking glass I was able to spot the ARS-7 still tied up at the dock. I could see smoke coming from her stack so I knew the engines were running and she was waiting for a passenger, ME. As I walked up the gang plank, I heard a voice from the bridge say . . . "single up all lines." I knew at that moment, I was on my way home to Pearl Harbor.

It took 16 days for the trip. When we arrived, I was able to call Nickie and give her the good news about my transfer. We decided during that call that our wedding day would be February 20, 1960.

Ships that were home ported in Pearl, were on what was called "Tropical Routine" in the Navy. The work day was 6:00 A.M. to 1:00 P.M. When you were off the ship, it was called LIBERTY; when on the ship every 3rd day, it was called having the DUTY. So, 2 off and 1 on, was the cycle. Being a radioman was kind of a soft job when on duty. I would check all incoming messages hourly pertaining to weather and any traffic related to a possible rescue Mission.

Some will recall the airplane crash off Martha's Vineyard, when John F. Kennedy Jr. along with his wife and sister in law, were all killed. The navy vessel assigned the task of retrieving the wreckage and bodies was the U.S.S. Grapple, (Formerly ARS-7), now ARS-53. The number was changed after a major overhaul and a re-commission into the fleet on the Atlantic side of the country, instead of the Pacific when I was stationed on her.

A point of interest: My wife and I are both licensed pilots and one of the last airplanes we owned and flew was one of the same, a 6-place **Piper Saratoga**. This craft is very much equipped with instruments for total instrument type trips. Why John Jr., a visual only licensed pilot would choose to fly this craft, is beyond me. I myself an instrument pilot found this plane to be a hand full when on long trips.

Saratoga

So, February 20th was to be the big day. Both Nickie and I had our work cut out for us. I had to find a furnished apartment on a bus route, so I could get back and forth to work. Nickie had to start sending me boxes of personal things, clothes, etc. and make airline reservations and arrive no later then February 14th. My Mother decided to come with Nickie since I needed my mother's signature to get married. Nickie was 19 years old and I was 20. The legal age for women in Hawaii was 18 but for men it was 21. Didn't seem right but, who am I to question the law of our new state of Hawaii?

All of the pieces were beginning to fit together. I picked them up at the Hawaiian International Airport on Sunday night, 6 days before the wedding.

Next was to find a Catholic priest and witnesses of the same faith. I remembered this task in INDY. I hoped it would be easier this time around and it was.

Wedding day

We were married at the **Submarine Navy Chapel** in **Pearl Harbor, Honolulu, Hawaii on February 20, 1960.** There was only 1 guest according to a photo taken by the Navy photographer - my mother. Back then, a young lady would not think about flying half way around the world, to marry without a proper chaperone. How things have changed.

We spent the rest of the afternoon driving around in an EDSEL rented car. You may wonder what was an EDSEL? It was a car brought out by the Ford Motor Company in the late 50/60's. We later took mother to the airport for her return flight home.

The honeymoon would last that night and the following day Sunday. It was kind of interesting because the apartment I rented was next door to an American Legion hall and they were having a party on our wedding night. We were not invited of course as they sang all of those patriotic songs very loudly, while they drank their beer. We survived and the next day we spent time at the beach together as husband and wife. It was our day to rejoice and thank the Lord for all our blessings. We know that He had a hand in making this happen. We were so happy.

The following day, Monday, Nickie had made a nice meal and was anxiously awaiting my arrival back from work. I had forgotten to tell her that I had the duty on the ship and would not be home until Tuesday afternoon. Since we had no phone, I asked a friend from the ship to stop by our house and tell her. Well, you can imagine what she was thinking: "He didn't like what he got this weekend and left me already." When my friend told her I had the duty on the ship, Nickie asked him: "What's the duty?" Ron said to her: "You married a sailor and you don't know what duty is? You have to be kidding!" Needless to say it was a tearful reunion on Tuesday but we worked through it.

It didn't take long for us to see that it would take more than a radioman's third class' pay to keep food on the table. So, Nickie went out and **found a job** with a land surveyor company the following day. She was very much liked and appreciated. They made a very nice 8 x 11 flyer and mailed it to all their customers, to introduce the new gal in the office. She looked very nice in her new job and surroundings.

Nickie at work

Living in Florida has allowed me to notice many 70 year old women and I have to say, my wife Nickie is probably the best preserved and looking of any I have seen thus far. She has kept her figure with only a few extra pounds in all the right places. I am so proud of her when I notice men of our generation looking at her with that eye, if you know what I mean.

I remember we bought a 53 Ford because we felt we just couldn't make it without our own transportation. It took 1 pregnancy and about 4 months, for us to realize we couldn't make it with the car either. It was sold right before she decided to return to Indiana to have our first child, while I went to Japan again for a 4 month tour. I was hoping to return in November and take a 30 day leave to be with Nickie. That I did and our new daughter **JoAnn Kay Bishop** was born on December 15th 1960, 2 weeks late.

JoAnn as baby

Nickie was allowed to come home from the hospital on the 18th and I had to leave on the 19th to return to my ship. Before I left, we named our daughter JoAnn. For a newborn child, she was really quite pretty. The next time I saw her, she was 2 months of age, when Nickie returned to Hawaii.

What happened next is almost unbelievable: Nickie got pregnant again! We started calling her "*Fertile Myrtle*". Our second daughter was born 12 months and 3 weeks after JoAnn.

Lynn as baby

For the birth of **Lynn Michele Bishop,** born on January 9th 1961, Nickie would be alone with the other gals at the apartment complex. I was notified while on watch at 2:00 A.M. while cruising in the Far East. All went well, I was told later. We lived in a pretty tight community and all of the women seemed to help each other, when their men were at sea for any extended period of time.

My four-year commitment to the U.S. Navy was coming to a close. Six months left and I felt sure I would not re-enlist. The only noteworthy event that occurred during this time was Nickie's attack of appendicitis. I was given a seven-day emergency leave to care for our daughters during her stay in the hospital. It was like I had a "*harem*" there at the apartment. I had women there to feed the girls, change diapers, bathe them and get them ready for bed. They would, believe it or not, sing to them until they fell asleep. Thank goodness I had this help. I'm not sure I could have done it by myself.

We left two weeks later on a Matts, a military owned aircraft, for San Francisco, CA. where I would receive my discharge. When we arrived, it took no time at all for the girls to catch a cold. The temperature change from Hawaii to this area was about 45 degrees and their little bodies just could not take it. Our immediate concern was to get them to Indiana where they could be cared for in a little bit of a warmer climate.

I went to the American Red Cross to ask for a loan to cover the expense of the airfare. They turned me down, flat. They said: "You're getting out of the service and how would we know you would repay us?" I couldn't believe it. Here I had been giving reluctantly to them for the last four years and when I needed help, this is how my family and I were treated. This was the day I decided to never again give a dime of my future income to this organization and I never have. My mother sent me $500 that night by Western Union and the girls and Nickie were on their way home the following morning.

Thirteen days later, I was officially discharged from the U.S. Navy. My car, the 1954 Chevrolet, was waiting for me in the receiving yard. It had been shipped four weeks earlier. I found a couple of guys looking for transportation to New York and agreed to give them a lift as far as Indiana, for their help with the driving. I would then take them to the bus station and they could complete their trip by Greyhound. It took two days for the drive and we all arrived safely. Was it ever good to be home! My stepfather Jimmy took the guys to the bus station for me. I rested and just watched my two little girls sleeping. They were so beautiful and I was so proud. What more could a man ask for? I was free from my commitment of serving my country, had a beautiful wife and 2 healthy children. I was ready to start what some would call a normal life with them, AFTER some rest, though.

I had no regrets for serving my country while in the Navy. It was 4 years of learning many things about being an adult and becoming a responsible person. When I enlisted, I was a pimple-faced kid of 18 years of age and look at me now. I did all this in such a short time. Just think of what we can accomplish in the next 50 years, or so.

In my sort of private way, I thanked the good Lord for blessing me with all I had received from Him. I felt free, loved and next to God in my plans for our future life together.

I look at our society today and I hope those politicians got a lot of votes for ridding our country of the military draft. It's probably one of the biggest mistakes of man in the 20th century.

A point of interest: Two of our grand-children have joined the Military voluntarily and for this, we are very proud.

CHAPTER THREE
"BACK TO BEING A CIVILIAN"

Now what? We'll get a few days rest and then plan to make the trip to Canada to introduce the girls to their grandparents, aunts, uncles and cousins.

It's good being home. The girls seemed to have gotten over their colds pretty quick so we will head to Canada, in a few days, about 1200 miles of easy driving. This will give Nickie and I a chance to talk about what we will be doing in the next few years while the girls sleep their normal 8 to 10 hours at night.

We got a lot of strange looks driving the old 1954 Chevy with the Hawaiian license plate. One older fellow asked: "How did you get that car over here?" I told him we had taken the new bridge. He just sort of stood there and shook his head as he said: "Things are moving too fast for me." We both laughed acknowledging the joke and went on our separate ways.

We had a safe enjoyable trip. We had left around 4:00 P.M. and drove until dark before stopping for a bite to eat. Nickie then asked the waitress to dampen a washcloth, so she could wash the little faces before they went to bed for the night. We arrived in the Montreal area in the early afternoon of the next day.

We had called ahead and they were standing on the front porch awaiting our arrival. Were they ever excited to see the girls and of course their daughter that had defied them, when she married me. It mattered not because we all expressed the love we had for each other and that is what was important.

After we got the suitcases inside, the relatives began to arrive. Jean-Claude, Nickie's older brother; Rita, her older sister and her little sister, Michele, who we named our 2nd daughter after.

The arrival was as it should have been. Everyone was really excited to see their NICOLE who had been kidnapped by this "*fast talking*" American sailor, 2 ½ years earlier. You see, they too had heard the saying about "*a girl in every port.*"

Let me be the first to tell you, that's just not true. It's sort of like, "*Davey Jones' Locker.*" That's not true either. Sailors are really nice people. My grandson Christopher recently joined the U.S. Navy and he is one of the nicest young people you could ever hope to meet.

Before I forget it, I just wanted to say that everyone accepted me and that meant so much. It's not often you can do what I did, like playing a role of the *"Knight in Shinning Armor"* and get away with it.

Writing this auto biographical book has made me realize just how blessed I had been to this point in my life. For this, I am very grateful. I'm sure I will try to be a better person because of it.

Nickie's aunt & uncle, Pauline & J.P.

Nickie's favorite **Aunt Pauline** was not there for the arrival, she and **her husband, Jean-Paul** were at their summer camp, a few miles away. So after a couple days' rest, we went to visit them with some of the cousins. All of the kids really enjoyed playing in the pool together while we the adults talked over the last 2½ years of our life in Hawaii.

A point of interest: It's November 11, 2011 and I'm in the process of editing this first book I've written, page by page. Aunt Pauline who is now 87 years of age and alone, likes to call us on SKYPE with VIDEO calling, at least once a week. It's good for Nickie, because it sort of keeps her up to date with what's going on with the family up north. She too likes news with what is happening in Florida. Of all the relatives, she was my favorite and we will always keep in touch. I'm sure it's lonely for her, now that Jean-Paul is gone, but we will keep a line of communication open as long as she is with us.

Getting back to the summer of 1962, I believe we spent about 6 or 7 days in total, before we headed back to Indianapolis. We had lots to do and of course I had to find work. No more of that easy life in paradise for me.

My father-in-law had suggested I contact a company that he had worked for while in Indianapolis, going to Chiropractic School. They manufactured and sold window coverings along with the installation services.

Before checking this out, I decided to contact a Naval Mfg. plant located in Indianapolis, where my Mother had retired from, years before. After 4 years of active service in the Navy, you would think they would have a job for me, if there were any jobs to be had. Was I naïve or what? I was offered a position as a night guardsman with a salary of $65 per week. I earned more then this while in the Navy, as an E-5 Radioman Second class petty officer. It was bad enough having the American Red Cross turn me down when I needed to get my sick daughters home to be cared for, but this? It was an insult to me and my family. Thanks but no thanks. Off to the drapery company my father-in-law had mentioned to me. I was hired at $65 per week here also but I was supplied with a Chevy El Camino car/truck to drive as my own. In it I carried all the necessary tools to do my job as an installer. Each day when given job assignments, I would place all the draperies and blinds that were to be installed that day in the back. It worked out fine.

Next thing was to find a place to live. We rented half of a double on North Kitley Avenue, located on the northeast side of the city. We bought one of those furniture packages for something like $899 for 4 rooms. Not really fine furniture but it would do the job for the first few years. I remember buying a washer and dryer from SEARS for less than $300 total. Try doing that today. We had all that was needed with a few exceptions, like a baby bed, a single bed and a couple of nightstands. We went to one of those seedy auctions in a shady part of town, on a Saturday night. Probably paid twice what it was worth.

We were still young and really not seasoned to what was going on in the outside world. Outside of the military, that is. Young and innocent, that's who we were.

By September, it seemed as though we had just about everything needed to begin our new life, with one exception. Remember that older car we brought back from Hawaii? Well it didn't have a heater and/or defroster, as these were not items needed for a car in the islands of Hawaii, with an average temperature of 86 F, year round.

Next thing I can recall is the purchase of a red and white Mercury hardtop and it did have a heater and defrosters, when it ran that is, which seemed not to be too often. The only thing this car had going for itself was, it was a nice looking car when cleaned up.

I was now a drapery and venetian blind installer in my first week of employment. The first couple weeks I rode with other installers learning the trade, as they say. The company was the Aero Drapery Company on Senate Avenue in Indianapolis, IN. It wasn't a bad job but I was always looking for something better as most young men usually do. The hardest part of the job was having "*old ladies*" watching every move you made while in their home. I reached a point when I didn't feel safe being alone with some of them.

I decided to seek a job where I could not have been accused of something immoral or whatever. I understood Aero was later sold to an Ohio firm, in a similar line of business. Was I ever glad I had left the company! I guess it was a real job moving an entire plant from one state to another.

Here we were the typical American family! Dad works all day, wife and mother takes care of the children and on Friday, we go on our weekly trip to the local A&P grocery store for food and things. Once a month, we allowed ourselves a trip to the Dairy Queen for treats with the girls.

I loved my wife and family but, I must admit I found myself asking: "Is this all there is?" I don't believe I was what you would call a "*happy camper*" (a term I would learn in later life). I think it was this first civilian job that helped me to feel this way. Those older rich ladies with their big houses, sort of did me in.

I resigned. No longer working in the drapery business and feeling a lot safer, as a result. I recalled being told by the Navy recruiter that my old job would be waiting when I returned, should I decide not to reenlist after my 4 years.

So guess what I did? I went to my local A&P grocery store and was working the following day, as a Dairy Products manager.

My job was rotating all of the dairy products on a daily schedule, grinding coffee beans and converting 50-pound cheese blocks into 1-pound packages, for sale. This cheese thing became a real job, so I designed, with a piece of piano wire and a 2x2 piece of ¾ inch plywood, a cutting board that really simplified the process. I enjoyed the job very much, even though the pay was not much more than before. I think it was something like $70 a week.

You know, looking back, I find it hard to believe we had to be below what is considered Middle class today. Oh yes, we paid our rent, electric bill, water bill, and payment on our furniture purchases. How in the world did we do it? No wonder I said "*Is this all there is*"? I just asked Nickie: "How did we survive?" She remembered the rent was $65 so it was 25% of our gross income as the economists say it should be. The only way from here was UP! I was determined to find it.

Well, at the time I was happy to have this job where I got to meet lots of fine people each week. And no one was looking over my shoulder all the time.

During the next few weeks, we started getting ready for our first winter in many years. We stayed inside a lot more, watched TV with the girls and played little girl games. I recall we had a small black and white TV that had a problem. The picture tube was about to go out and it only showed 2/3 of a normal picture. I can't recall how long it was before it finally did conk out. But I do remember that fellow on "Gunsmoke" was a lot taller then I had thought. As a matter of fact, everything looked bigger when we replaced it. The things I remember are beginning to amaze me.

What happened next is a little foggy in my memory. For some reason, we went back to Canada to see Nickie's parents. Why, I do not know. Here we were with a CAR that was unreliable, 1200 miles of hard driving before us, in the dead of winter. I must have had a brain fade or something of that nature.

The trip was pretty good until we crossed the border in Detroit, MI. It started snowing and it continued for the next 600 miles, as we crossed the Ontario Province into Quebec. Thank goodness we were on the Canadian Hwy #401, so the road was in excellent condition and the plows were going after it. One thing I can say for Canada is they know what to do, when it snows. During the entire trip in Canada, we did not see a single accident. That would never happen in the Midwest. Cars would be all over the place if 6 inches of snow would have fallen.

Like I said, this part of the story is still foggy in my mind at remembering what happened some 48 years ago. I knew we were not very happy with our lives, since coming home from the Navy. Even though we were now all together as a family, which was wonderful, it just didn't seem like enough. Oh yes, as I said before, we could pay the bills but there was absolutely nothing left, for the toys little girls liked to play with, a night out or a meal in a nice restaurant once in a while.

Four years in the United States Navy and this is what my life had become. No, I was not at all happy. I would have gone anywhere for a chance to do better and this is probably what enticed me to make the trip to Canada, in the dead of winter.

At some point it was decided and agreed upon by the two of us, that we would live in Canada for a few years. Trying to get a better handle on what it was that we really wanted from life. I knew I could do better for them, if I could get a job with some kind of a future.

Grandma and Grandpa Marcoux now lived in a little white frame house facing the river. It was a beautiful setting with circular driveway in front.

My Father-in-law was telling me about a company down the road (5 miles or so), called United Aircraft of Canada, Ltd. Supposedly they were in the process of developing a new smaller type turbo-prop engine for customers such as: Beech Aircraft Corp, Bell Helicopters and others. Because they were an American owned and operated company, they should have a lot of employment opportunities for English speaking people such as myself, I thought. It was like a breath of fresh air had blown my way. I got all excited and very hopeful for the first time since coming home from the service.

Before leaving for Indianapolis, I drove down to Longueuil where the plant was and filled out an application, asking if an interview could be arranged for the afternoon, as we were on our way back to Indiana.

This plant had previously manufactured cylinders and pistons for the Pratt and Whitney Engine Company of Connecticut, in the USA. Their engine, the WASP was like the "*grand daddy*" of WWII and after. Many thousands of this type engine are still in use today. They were now in the preliminary stages of reworking the plant layout to bring in new equipment for the building of this new engine.

Once this engine was coming off the production line, they would then need to hire some Test Technicians to get them certified for TBO (time between overhaul) times. That's where I could fit in, if hired.

The General Manager of this operation was quite impressed with my background in the Navy. I had the experience with instruments and electronic gear that he was looking for and I was English speaking and educated. I told him that we had decided to return to Canada, for a few years, giving me a chance to get to know my wife's family and to possibly find a better job then the one back in Indiana. "We should be ready in about 6 to 9 months from now, to fire up our test cells. Then there will be a job here, for you, if still interested." I let him know, I would be. He asked that I keep in touch and call him when settled.

Basically, we had already decided that we would live in Canada for a few years, so this just sort of "*put the icing on the cake*". For the first time since leaving the Navy, I could see that there maybe a better life for my family and I was very happy about this.

Nickie's sister Rita

So, I was to return to Indiana and apply for a Visa, to live in Canada, sell this unreliable car and get another. We needed to have a trailer hitch installed and wait for the Visa to be approved. Then rent a trailer and bring all of our belongings back to Canada to our new apartment. It was decided that Nickie would go back with me and her older **sister Rita** would take care of Lynn and her mom would take care of JoAnn, until we returned.

After a tearful goodbye, Nickie and I were driving south again to Indianapolis. When we arrived, telling Mother and Jimmy of our decision to move back to Canada, actually went better then I could have expected. They understood that we both wanted something better for our family and were quite gracious about our decision.

After a couple days' rest, we laid out our plans and put everything into motion. We would both work while attempting to save as much money as possible. I remember Nickie leaving the house early one morning telling me she would have a job when she returned. It was times like this when I realized just how lucky of a man I was to have such a wife and mother for our children. When she returned, she did have a job. She was to work at Household Finance Company in downtown Indianapolis.

Time flew by as we made all of the preparations for our move. We missed the girls and of course, were anxious to see them again. As mentioned before, we both had fulltime jobs and this helped to make the time move by a little quicker than usual.

April 1st, 1963. This was the day we left my parents driveway and ran out of GAS before reaching the corner. We all got a good laugh. Jimmy said: "And you're going to drive all the way to Montreal, Canada?" This was the plan and I knew that with God's help, we would make it O.K.

This was to be our chance at a new life, a better life, that is.

CHAPTER FOUR
"STARTING A "NEW" LIFE"

Well, we were now in Canada. Kind of ironic I thought, I serve 4 years in the United States Navy and end up in Canada looking for a future, with a decent paying job. United Aircraft was not yet ready to start hiring for the test cells. It was still a few months away.

Thank goodness Nickie's parents had the foresight to find and rent an apartment for us. What would we have done with a trailer load of belongings, had they not? For some reason, it is like yesterday. 36 De Niverville Street, Boucherville, Quebec, was the address of our new home. It was a nice little community, next to the St. Lawrence River.

We unloaded and placed all of the furniture in their perspective rooms and sat down for a rest. Lots of things left to do with a move of this magnitude. I played with the girls for a couple days before heading out, looking for employment to tide us over for a few months.

This is when I learned what it would be like, to not be bilingual in the province of Quebec, while looking for a job. After applying at probably 25 different locations, a thought hit me.

English Ford Anglia

Why not go back to A&P? I felt sure they must have stores in the Montreal area. One such store on the west side catered to mostly English speaking Canadians. This was working out better then I had expected. Believe-it-or-not, I was hired to be the Dairy Department Manager. The only drawback was the location of the store, 21 miles west of Boucherville. That meant a 42 mile round trip every day. I needed to get a different car that would give me some better mileage than I was presently getting. I had seen a car about the size of a VW the day before with a for sale sign attached. Turns out, this was a 4 cylinders **English Ford Anglia** that gets around 40+ miles per gallon, runs good and tires looked O.K. The price was $400 cash. I have no idea where we got the money but we bought the car that very day.

It was a good little car and it served our needs perfectly. We even drove it to Indianapolis for a long Thanksgiving weekend. I had Friday, Saturday, Sunday and Monday off and we drove almost 2400 miles to eat turkey with my family.

While there, my uncle Tex who was a professional truck driver, looked over my purchase and decided we needed tires, before heading back home. We met at the Blue and White truck garage in Indy and 4 new tires were installed. The tires were only 13 inch so, if I remember right, they were not expensive and we paid him shortly after arriving back home.

Oh to be that YOUNG and that STUPID is enough to scare the wits out of one's person. 80 MPH was the normal speed on the 600-mile stretch of Hwy 401 that went between Detroit and Montreal. We averaged this type mileage on most of the trip and now we are told we need new tires before driving back. The more I write in this book, the more I realize that GOD has been watching over my family and me for quite some time.

Things were beginning to look a little brighter in our lives. This was about the time that Nickie found a job working for a Land Surveying Company. This sure helped out with the paying of the bills. We had not hit the jackpot YET but it made life a lot easier and we could do more for each other as well as for the girls.

At first, Nickie's mother took care of the girls but this eventually got to be too tiring for her. She too was a Chiropractor, as was my father-in-law. They sort of worked as a team in the office and having a couple little ones disturbing them all the time just got to be too much.

We then found a young girl, maybe 16 or so, that would live with us and care for the girls. We basically made her a part of our family. When we went somewhere, she went with us.

Almost 6 months had passed. I was still at the A&P and enjoying talking and working with all the English folks.

You see, at the family gathering, I was always the one sitting off to the side, that couldn't speak French. I must admit that most of the relatives tried as best they could but I knew it was a struggle for them and I chose to not put them in that uncomfortable position. It was not as bad as it sounds. After being there for almost a year, I usually could follow most of the conversation and when something came up that I wanted to say, I just said it and the ones that could understand, then they would translate to the others.

About this time, we got a phone call from United Aircraft of Canada Ltd. I had filled out an application there over a year ago. After this much time I figured they had thrown away my application for employment so it was a pleasant surprise to hear from them. They wanted to talk to me about my Navy training and then offer me a job. For some reason, I told them I was leaving on vacation and would contact them on my return. I thought Nickie was going to have a heart attack.

At A&P, I was making $70/wk and driving 42 miles round trip each day. They were offering $425/mo and the plant was less then 5 miles from Boucherville, where we lived. I sure am glad they waited for me to contact them. If not, I think my wife would have left me. Just kidding of course!

We were so happy that we called my family to let them know the good news and they also talked to the girls. Mother was very happy for us and gave me some good advice. She said: "Work hard and learn well, you'll be a valued employee, before you know it."

By-the-way, both girls, JoAnn and Lynn, were totally bilingual by now. This was about the time in history when the French Separatist movement in the province of Quebec was trying to separate from the rest of Canada and have their own country. This was a very nasty movement for the government.

We used to call Lynn, our youngest daughter, our "*little separatist*" because she would not speak English to me, even though she knew how.

This is what the movement was all about. I think it is still going on, as I am writing this book. The idea is to have a French speaking country. If you were not French speaking then, you were not welcome. If you are visiting the country, however, you are always more than welcomed and most find French Canadians very warm and friendly.

I accepted the job and worked in the test cells helping to certify a new type of turboprop aircraft engine. For some reason, I felt like I was on my way to something better.

I continued my employment there for almost 5 years before returning to Indianapolis to raise our children. By this time we had added another member to our family Bryan Robert Bishop. He was 4 months old and his papa's pride and joy!

You might wonder why it was that we left Canada and moved back to my home state. There were lots of reasons but probably the most obvious one was, winters in Canada are horrible. Sub-Zero temperatures for weeks at a time, is hard to get used to. The Separatist movement was getting stronger and things and attitudes against the English were getting worse.

Example: The French wanted everything to be bilingual all across Canada. Ottawa, the nation's capital, rather then lose Quebec to the country, went along with it. If you ever traveled in Canada, you will notice that everything is Bilingual in only 9 provinces. Quebec didn't go along with the change. They just demanded it for everyone else except themselves. When driving up to visit my wife's family, I have had to get Nickie to read the signs for me, so I won't get lost.

In schools, the primary language was French. Our two girls were being educated in English however but when JoAnn was in the first grade, there were some issues, regarding the reward system, for doing good work. My wife actually offered to buy the stickers to put on our daughter's papers which embarrassed the teacher to the point that she started acknowledging the good work that JoAnn had been doing.

For those that know little about elementary education, let me tell you from personal experience that this type of a teacher will actually destroy a child's interest in being educated. From this day forward, JoAnn (who became Andrea's mother in later life) hated school and would actually take summer classes so she could graduate early.

I never regretted moving to Canada for a few years because, even though it was not a good move financially, it was a good move for our relationship, our marriage and family. I got to know Nickie's family better, their way of doing things and basically how she was raised, their values and their affection for each other. I mentioned to my wife at one time that her family and friends were the most kissing people I had ever encountered since they kissed all the time. That's the *FRENCH* in them!

I never regretted for a minute my decision to leave Canada and return to Indiana, either. We had bought a house by then so we sold it along with our car and left with a Ryder truck, full of our possessions, in August 1968.

CHAPTER FIVE
"BACK HOME AGAIN"

Once we got back to Indiana, our first concern was to get the girls in school and this became a problem for JoAnn. It was felt that she was not up to U.S. standards to go into the 3rd grade and they wanted to place her back into the 2nd grade. I remember the night like it happened yesterday. JoAnn cried her little eyes out. I had never witnessed her in so much pain and all we could do was hug and comfort her. She promised to do whatever was necessary so this would not happen.

We agreed to have her go to the 3rd grade, as was our option. With a lot of help and homework, she passed and went on to the 4th and so on until she graduated at mid-year, at the age of 16. She had never failed a grade and usually excelled in all subjects even thou we knew how much she had been negatively influenced by that 1st grade teacher, in Canada.

Shortly after her graduation, she tells us that she wants to go to Canada and live with her aunt Michele, Nickie's younger sister. We realized sometime back that she is now into drugs, probably smoking pot and such. I'm sure that her thought was to get away from our supervision or to put it more frankly, we knew her too well and maybe Michele could be fooled for a time. This arrangement didn't go too well and I understand that JoAnn had met a guy and they were now living together. I guess Michele was more aware then we thought. This situation didn't work out either and I remember having a hitch installed on our family car and renting a trailer to bring her things home again.

Here is a SYNOPSIS of what followed, in later years in JoAnn's life: after returning home she met a fellow named Danny. They were soon married and it turns out that the 2 of them did drugs together and he abused her physically.

After the divorce, JoAnn needed another change and moved to Florida to live with Nickie's parents in a home we had provided for them in Clearwater, for their retirement years.

This arrangement never worked, as she would not follow some simple rules, like coming in at a reasonable time at night. They loved their granddaughter and worried a lot about her wellbeing and they themselves were unable to get a good night's rest, worrying about her.

Next, she met a fellow named Eric from Texas. He happened to be vacationing in Florida. Next thing we knew she was off to Texas and then to Denver, Colorado. At some point, they broke up and she moved back home in Indiana. Eric showed up later at our home to patch things up. They got things worked out and JoAnn asked if our minister could marry them in our church. Then back to Colorado they went. Various telephone calls indicated that the marriage was not going well. That old "*demon*" popped its ugly head again: physical abuse, drugs, booze. This marriage was doomed to fail as were the others.

American Trans Air (ATA) announced that they were about to have an inaugural flight to Denver. We had been members with the Ambassador Air Flying Club for many years so we bought a couple of tickets. What good we thought we could do, is beyond me.

Here's what happened. After a few days there, we were waiting for Eric to return home from work. Around 7:00PM or so, we started getting hungry for supper and a phone call told us that Eric would not be coming home, as he was stone drunk. This was when she would get most of the abuse she said, so I told her to pack a bag and she was coming with us to the Holiday Inn for supper and a good night's sleep. We would return to INDY the next morning.

If any of you reading this, have been through this before, you can see that I was a big enabler for my daughter. I realized this some years later but also had to forgive myself since all was done because of the love I had for her. I would often ask myself: "What more could I do to try and straighten her life out?"

So here we are, back in Indianapolis and we have a daughter living in our home again. JoAnn found a good job at United Student Aid Funds and things seemed to be going pretty well. One night she came home around 3 or 4 a. m. and we had it out, right then and there: "You live in my house and you follow my rules." It wasn't long after that that she found an apartment and we helped her get it set up. It was a nice little place, which she shared with a fellow worker from USAF.

A few months passed and JoAnn met a guy named TOM. He was a piano player at a club in INDY and quite a nice fellow. They dated for a few months and had a beautiful outdoor wedding. Both bride and groom looked very happy. They rented a home on the south side of the city in a nice neighborhood with children. It wasn't long before our daughter was also expecting a child. It was really a wonderful time in our lives with JoAnn. Being pregnant was important to her and Tom and she swore off drugs during the 9 months it took to create this wonderful little boy named Christopher. By the way, this grandson is now fully grown and has enlisted in the U.S. Navy and hopes to become a Navy SEAL.

Things were good and JoAnn was doing a good job being the loving mother. Shortly after Christopher's birth, Tom was offered a really good opportunity to open up a piano bar club in St Charles, Missouri. By this time, I had begun my career as a salesman for a company that manufactured conveyor belt fasteners and a part of my territory was St. Louis of which, St Charles was a suburb. I was usually in the area every 2 to 3 weeks and that was great.

Things seemed to be going good but we kept hearing about JoAnn going to bed depressed and staying there for days at a time. She was back on the anti-depressant medications again. I, her father, knew all too well where this was going to lead my daughter and her family.

In an attempt to get help, Tom demanded they go to a counselor. I really do not think this was of any help because soon after this started Nickie and I were accused of sexual abuse. It gets worse. They met a young female lawyer who wanted to make a name for herself and she along with Tom and JoAnn filed a law suit against us asking for 1 million $$ in damages. She charged them no fee, I was told later. She was only after the publicity since this was the first time that such a lawsuit of its kind was ever filed in the State of Missouri. All of them appeared on their local news channel.

This was at a time when the rage in the therapy business was, if you're having any problems in your young life, blame your parents and use what was then a new term appropriately called: "False Memory Syndrome." It got very nasty and the suit was eventually dropped as there was no truth in it. The next time I laid eyes on my daughter was actually 8 years later.

Every once in a while I will have someone ask: "Don't I know you?" This is probably because we, my wife and I appeared on ABC's Nightline program and had an opportunity to defend ourselves. JoAnn, her mother and I had 12 minutes to say whatever we wanted.

When ABC called us to let us know that our interview would be televised the following Friday, I called all my colleagues from work and most of our friends, to let them know. We did not want anyone seeing this without being aware of what was happening in our family. Our interview was done at our home in Carmel, Indiana, a suburb of Indianapolis and theirs was done in St. Charles, Mo. I actually watched my daughter tell all of America, how much she loved her Dad. From the interview, it was quite easy to see just how confused she really was.

We received many calls from friends and even some strangers, to let us know that they were shocked by her accusation and believed us and were standing by us. How comforting and heart warming. Not one relative or friend believed her or turned against us.

A couple of years later, we heard from a mutual friend that JoAnn, her husband and son had moved to Florida. We missed her terribly but had been told by her and her therapist that we were not to make contact with her, that she needed time to heal.

Four years later, we received a call from her husband Tom. As soon as Nickie answered, he said: "I wouldn't blame you if you never wanted to talk to me again but I felt that I needed to talk to you. I don't believe anymore that Jerry molested JoAnn. She just sued me for divorce and has accused me of molesting our son. It is not true and I am going to fight those charges because I want custody of our son. The false allegation has helped me to realize that the accusation against you is false also and I am so sorry for ever believing her."

Nickie and I were getting ready to go on a cruise, departing from Fort Lauderdale and since they didn't live very far from there, Nickie asked him if it would be possible to meet with him and see our grandson since we had not seen him for such a long time. Nickie's aunt Pauline and her husband were spending their winters in Florida, close to Ft. Lauderdale, so they made arrangements to see each other while Nickie was visiting her aunt.

A week later, I flew in and Tom, Christopher and Nickie picked me up at the airport and he took us both to the dock where the cruise ship was anchored. They had had a nice visit and Tom had even left Christopher to spend the night with Nickie, her aunt and uncle, while he went to work. You can imagine how much this little guy had grown since we had last seen him. At the time, he was 4 months old and he was now 4 years old.

Eventually, Tom won custody of Christopher. When Chris was 6 years old, Tom let him fly to Indy and he spent a week with us. We had a really good time getting to know him and he got to meet his uncle Bryan and some of his cousins. We heard later that JoAnn had found out about our visit to Florida and had approved of Chris visiting us. Were her feelings toward us changing?

After almost 8 years of no contact between us, Nickie got an e-mail from her wishing us a Happy Thanksgiving and writing us that she missed us and missed her Grandma Kay's pecan pies. Nickie answered her, wished her the same and assured her of our love for her. They continued to e-mail each other for almost a year before we actually got to see her again. In her e-mails, she often asked about other family members, wanting to know how they were and be brought up to date about them.

In June, she called one evening and when Nickie answered the phone she asked to speak to me and asked her to stay on the line. As soon as I answered, after asking me how I was, she told me how sorry she was for the accusation and could I ever forgive her? Of course, I did and then asked her how had she finally come to this realization? She told me that she had been seeing a new counselor and he had made her realize that it couldn't possibly be true, that the counselor in

St. Louis had made her believe this in order for her to heal the pain.

Finally, after much correspondence back and forth, Nickie asked her if she wanted to come and see us. She immediately accepted and came to see us in September of that year. It was so good to see her after all those years. Nothing about the accusation was ever mentioned or talked about.

We kept in touch by phone or e-mail and after finding out that I was retiring in November, JoAnn mentioned to her mother that they should have a surprise retirement party for me. Can you imagine the shock of seeing my daughter, when the crowd in my driveway separated and there in the center stood our 3 children, JoAnn, Lynn and Bryan?

Nickie, and JoAnn had actually located all of the people that played a part in my life for the past 25 years and they were there. Thank goodness we had a large home because it was quite a large group. It was great seeing some of the people from Amway. This business had been a part of our lives since 1969. We also had raced USAC type full midget racing cars for some 6 years or so and then took up flying. After I got my private pilot's license, Nickie decided to get her private license, while I continued on with getting my instrument license.

We had started an airplane rental company named, JERNIK Aviation Inc. and during a 6 years' period had a total of 9 planes of all shapes and sizes that were rented out for various purposes and tasks. So as you can see, we had a very busy life and tried to do things that would include the entire family.

In editing what I've written so far, I noticed that I have talked very little about our other 2 children, Lynn and Bryan. Sorry about that, "KIDS".

Lynn

Remember, **Lynn** was born approximately 1 year after JoAnn at Tripler Army Hospital in Honolulu, Hawaii. She takes after my wife's side of the family. Dark hair and light complexion. She was my little "*separatist*" I talked about earlier. She was basically a good student and never inclined to use drugs. After high school, she went back to school and became a phlebotomist. She worked at a hospital nearby until she decided that she wanted to move to Florida. She could not stand the cold winters anymore.

Lynn & Brad

She is a good mother and is married to a very nice man **Brad** that works with the fire department here in Florida. Brad has two sons, Michael and Christopher and Lynn has three sons Matthew, Thomas, Ethan and a daughter, Ciara. Her oldest son Matthew is in the Army and has been in Iraq twice. Knowing he was leaving for Iraq again last summer, he and his fiancée decided to get married. When he got back this past August, they had the very nice wedding she had always dreamed of having and renewed their vows in September. Needless to say, we are very proud of him.

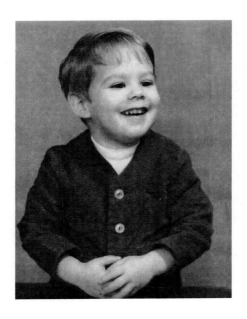

Young Bryan

Our third child is a young man named **Bryan**. Bryan like most of his generation played around with drugs but not to the extent of his sister JoAnn. He too is married to a really nice lady named **Mindi** and they have 2 little girls, Molli and Graci. Bryan has a son named Jeremy who graduated from college this year and was our first grandson. He also has an older daughter, now 17 years old, named Sadie.

Bryan & Mindi

I could not be more proud to call him my son. He is a professional musician and plays the night club scene 2 to 3 nights per week. Told me the other day, he believed he has the best band in all of the Indianapolis area. He actually taught himself a number of instruments and writes a lot of the music they use in their act.

Bryan, Lynn & JoAnn

So there you have it. Jerry and Nicole Bishop, parents of 3 beautiful children, **JoAnn, Lynn and Bryan**; ten grandchildren: Jeremy, Matthew, Thomas, Christopher, Ethan, Sadie, Ciara, Andrea, Molli, and Graci.

This generation has been no easier for us to raise then most reading this book has experienced and/or will experience in the future.

CHAPTER SIX
"JOANN'S STORY"

Eight years is a long time to not talk to someone you care about. I had almost gotten used to the idea of never seeing my daughter again and all of a sudden, here she is at my retirement party. What's next? I thought. The next morning, she asked Nickie and I go to the living room. She had something important she wanted to tell us.

She was PREGNANT. The father is the result of a one night stand and he is not giving our daughter the impression that he really wants anything to do with a child. Why should he? Who says it is his child, anyway? How many other men were there in her life at the time, anyway?

The next day we took JoAnn to the airport for her trip back home. While waiting, she asked her mother and I, if we would allow her to return home to have her baby. I reminded her that it was not I who decided she should leave our home, some 8 years earlier. The door was never closed then and it is not closed now. So, the answer is yes, but you live in our home, you follow our rules. NO DRUGS. She assured us that this would not happen. The health of the unborn was more important to her and I believed her as this was to be her 2nd child and I recalled that this was her own set of rules for the 9 months of her first pregnancy also. I knew that JoAnn meant what she had said. I hoped we could have a few months together and be able to function as a family, for a change. I hoped and prayed this would happen and it did. As we suspected, the father of the child wanted nothing to do with the situation. He had his night of so-called fun and that was all he had really been interested in anyway.

It wasn't long after this that we made a trip to Wilmington, NC to pick-up her belongings, which included a rather large Collie dog named FRED. She was coming home and I must admit that I was happy about it. I loved my daughter and I had missed her during those 8 years of separation. Since we had just built a new "so called retirement home" we had plenty of room for her and the child. We even had room for Fred.

For the next few months we went through a pretty hard winter and it was not an easy time for any of us. We had lots of snow and freezing rain. JoAnn and I took turns walking Fred. As much as I had sworn to never have a dog around again, it was sort of nice having old Fred. He and I became pretty good friends during the following months.

Four months or so into the pregnancy, an examination indicated that the child JoAnn was carrying was a girl and would be born with Down Syndrome (DS). I recall this time being a very tense time in our home. Many decisions would have to be made before the child arrived. JoAnn didn't seem to know what to do. Thank goodness we had raised her well enough to exclude abortion, as an option.

During the following months, we all tried to educate ourselves about DS on the Internet, before her birth. JoAnn realized that she would be alone to raise this child and decided to get in touch with an Adoption Agency. A representative from the agency came over and brought letters from four Christian families ready to adopt her knowing that she would be born with DS. JoAnn being eight month's pregnant at the time, knew her hormones were playing havoc with her body and mind and it was not the right time to be making such an important decision. She told the representative that she would give her final answer after her child was born.

Secretly, I wanted this child. She wasn't just a special child with "*Special Needs*" but a special Gift from GOD. I wanted her more than I had ever wanted anything in my entire life. I knew that GOD had protected us for a reason and I felt that she WAS that reason.

The day finally arrived on May 28th, 2001 and Andrea was born. When she was cleaned up by the birthing nurse, she was laid on her mother's chest and that did it. JoAnn would never part with this child, from that day forward, "we thought". She was a beautiful child and I had prayed so much all these months that she would not be given away in adoption.

I remember going to the hospital the first time, shortly after her birth, Andrea was in an incubator and had tubes running out of almost every cavity of her little body. I was told that she had a breathing/eating disorder. She was being fed intravenously and this went on for the following 19 days.

At some point, enough was enough. We, her grandma and grandpa along with JoAnn basically demanded that we be allowed to take her home. The hospital staff was not really happy with our decision but what could they do? They told us that we had to keep feeding intravenously. We found out later that they had been charging Medicaid $1000/day for her stay. We always wondered if this was the reason they wanted to keep her.

As soon as we got her home, the first thing was to take out the feeding tube, which JoAnn and her mom did very carefully. It was like a miracle! She flourished and immediately started eating and gaining weight. She was my bundle of joy and I held her as often as possible.

She was such a beautiful child and something would happen to me every time I held her. It was a feeling of true love that I had experienced only one other time, before her birth. It's like when I met Nickie, back in 1959. I knew right away that this was the woman I would spend the rest of my life with. And by today's standards, a 52-year marriage is nothing to sneeze at. I made a choice then and I am just as sure of my feelings toward Andrea now.

I must admit, I didn't know at the time why GOD had sent us this blessed child. I was to find out some 4 years later though, while living in Southwest Florida.

As summer approached, JoAnn told us that she wanted to move to a warmer climate, because of her fibromyalgia, which was temperature sensitive. She had lived in Fort Lauderdale some years before and knew that the warmer weather would make her life more comfortable, as well as better for Andrea. We agreed with her but asked that she would live on the west side of the state, near the rest of our small family. This would allow us to help her get settled in and to also help with the care of Andrea. It would also give JoAnn some time to herself to try and put the pieces of her life back together. As I had recently retired, there was a strong possibility for us to be moving also. My mother and sister and her husband as well as our daughter Lynn with her family, all lived there and just loved the warm climate and activities all year around. We all agreed to move to Florida and we would now start the process of getting it accomplished.

Before moving on let me just say a few words about fibromyalgia. I had talked with our family doctor about this illness and he told me it was very hard to prove or disprove. I had a strong feeling this had something to do with her ability of getting so many pain relievers, whenever she wanted them. Had I known this before Andrea was born, the decision would have been made some time ago. With JoAnn addicted to pain medicine, there was no way she would be able to raise this child by herself and that I was sure of.

My sister had told me about a home across the street from where she lived that was for sale. The lady was moving back up north to Illinois to be near her daughter's family and her grandchildren. Since I was visiting my mom and sister in July, I liked the home so much that I sent Nickie some photos of it on the computer and bought it from the lady on the spot. It was a nice doublewide with 2 baths and 2 bedrooms along with a den, ideal for an office. A covered car port, screened in lanai and a beautiful flower bed that separated itself from a 10'x8' storage shed, that was perfect for a man's workshop. Priced at $70,000, it seemed to be a fair price and it was conveniently located. Our park was called Tara Woods.

In September 2001, JoAnn flew to Fort Myers to look around at the family parks in the area. Had we understood the Florida law better, JoAnn could have lived in a 55+ park with the rest of the family because "Special Needs" children were exempt from the 55-year old requirement. Then there was also her dog Fred. So the family park was the right choice after all. She decided on a park named Island Vista, located about 2 to 3 miles south of the 55+ park where we would be living. If I recall, she picked out a home from a park model. All we needed was the selling price to give to the bank in Noblesville, IN. and the loan would be put into motion. Her mother and I had been banking there for many years and knew the Vice-President quite well. He worked out a personal loan for her, with my signature as co-signer, for her new home. I recall the payments were in the neighborhood of $300 per month which she could easily afford.

With the help of my brother-in-law Bob, we built her 8 pieces of kit furniture. She now had a new home completely furnished. Bob and I had a lot of fun getting her all set up.

This move had become quite an adventure for the family. My wife had bought me a new Ford Sport Trac for my retirement and I decided since I had nothing else to do that I would buy an 8'x12' cargo trailer and move JoAnn and ourselves down to Florida. I made 3 round trips enjoying the time alone with my thoughts and dreams for our future.

Martha and Bob had let us store our belongings in their lanai until our home was ready to move into. Two or three weeks after we got JoAnn settled in, we moved to our new home. Had you lived down the street, you could of watched these crazy bunch of people running back and forth across the street carrying lamps and what ever goes in a home. It was a lot of fun and if the truth be known, we didn't save anything by doing all of this, ourselves.

The morning after completing the 3rd trip, Bob knew a fellow that wanted to buy my trailer. He was moving his family back to Kansas. I had bought it for $2300, made 3 round trips to Florida and would sell it for $1800. Not a bad deal when you think about it.

Andrea with mommy JoAnn

So here we were; Nickie and I living across the street from my sister, Martha and Bob in Tara Woods, my mother living in Punta Gorda at Emerald Lakes, 20 miles north and JoAnn with Andrea and Fred living at Island Vista, some 2 to 3 miles south of Tara Woods on Highway 41. Our daughter Lynn and Brad were living in Bushnell, FL and our son Bryan was still in Indiana.

There you have it. We were the typical American family. If I had to figure who we were, I'd say upper middle class. All of the 5 families mentioned, were not rich but not poor either. Happy and in love is the best description for all.

It is now August 12, 2004. You might wonder how is it that I remember this date? We are about to be hit with a hurricane named Charlie the next day, on Friday the 13th. It went right through Punta Gorda, where my mother lived. Thank goodness she was across the street with Martha and Bob. Her home was totally destroyed.

Remember the workshop I wrote about earlier? Experts had told us that the shed (workshop) was anchored in concrete, a lot better than the house so it was the safest place to be during a hurricane. So that is where Nickie and I, along with JoAnn and Andrea waited out the storm in N. Ft Myers. Our home actually had less then $100 damage. So as you can see, the storm was really some 20 miles north of us in Punta Gorda. Like most men, my workshop was very clean and well organized. I had laid out a blanket on the floor and Andrea thought we were having a party. She was too young to know or care as to what was going on outside. She was 3 years of age at the time.

This was about the time we began to notice that JoAnn was really hitting the pill bottles.

It seemed like every 20 to 30 minutes she was putting something in her mouth. Then her body would seem to go limp and she would lose semi-consciousness. Being together in an 8'x10' building for about 3 to 4 hours, waiting for the all clear from hurricane Charlie, sort of opened our eyes to what had been going on at her house, down the road.

Thank goodness we had set some rules and guidelines, regarding the care of Andrea that went like this. If either her mother or I saw any indication in her behavior that would indicate recent medicine or drug usage, JoAnn was not permitted to leave with Andrea. Before, something like this would have become an issue between us but not now. It was almost like JoAnn wanted to leave her with us. She could then do her thing, whatever that was.

Our life was really becoming almost unbearable. We were living like an alcoholic "one day at a time." We would wonder, what is going to happen next? An investigation that will take place later showed that during this period, we actually had Andrea 80 to 90% of the time.

January 2005, an old friend from Indianapolis who was now living in the state of Washington had contacted JoAnn and asked if she could come for a visit. Of course, JoAnn wanted to show off her beautiful daughter Andrea and asked if she could have her for the night. We dropped our guard and allowed this and the next thing we knew, we were getting a call from the local hospital that Andrea had been sexually molested and was in emergency waiting in the ER to be examined by a doctor.

When I got there, JoAnn had obviously taken a bunch of meds and was almost in a trance. Her friend was holding Andrea all wrapped up in a baby blanket to keep warm. It was a very chilly night and quite cold in the waiting area. We waited for what seemed like an eternity before she was called. I was stopped at the door and not allowed to accompany her to the examining room.

I was told that I had been accused by her mother and she didn't want me near her daughter, my granddaughter. Does this not sound familiar. . . False Memory Syndrome (FMS)? Is it creeping its ugly head into our lives again? How could JoAnn in her wildest imagination actually try to send us down this FMS road again? Accusing me her father, that would give his life for this child, of such a horrible crime. It was like reliving the past, when she had accused her mother and I of molesting her, when she was a child. I couldn't believe it was happening again. I thought this part of my life was over. Eight years of separation had obviously not taught JoAnn anything.

I stayed in the ER waiting room for a couple hours thinking that maybe someone would come to their senses. It didn't happen and I eventually went home. When I arrived, Nickie was at the kitchen table with a cup of coffee. I told her that I had again been accused of sexual molestation. This time against my granddaughter Andrea that I loved so much. Needless to say, Nickie was beside herself. After all that we had done to try and put our family back together and she does this again.

A couple of hours later, JoAnn called her mother to let her know that she was home with Andrea. Nickie asked her what happened but she answered that it was late and she was tired and going to bed. She also told her not to call her that she would call back when she had some rest. How could they (the hospital authority) let her take Andrea home with her? Anyone with half a brain could have seen that JoAnn was medicated to the hilt, especially trained people in the profession of medicine. Needless to say, we did not sleep very well or much that night, what was left of it.

Saturday evening, while watching TV with a family friend, Rosalyn from Indiana, who was visiting for a few days, there was a loud knock on the door. There were 2 persons, a detective from the Lee County Sheriffs' Department and a young lady from the Department of Children and Family Services (DCF).

After identifying themselves they asked if they could come in and speak to Nickie and I regarding our granddaughter Andrea. Of course I replied we have been hoping to talk to someone about this all day.

What happened next was a little nerve rattling. Nickie was asked to meet with John, the detective on the lanai, in the back part of the house and I was to talk with the young lady from DCF (I believe her name was Sally), in the living room.

Their questions were mainly about where Andrea was the day before, what had we done with her while in our care, etc. They both interviewed us separately. Then the sheriff spoke to both of us and told us that he believed us. In order to prove our innocence however, he asked us if we would be willing to take a lie detector test. We both agreed immediately and it was set up for the next afternoon on Sunday.

I did have a question for the DCF lady; that kind of put her back in her chair. It was: "Why did the hospital allow Andrea to return home with her mother, (who was obviously over medicated) and a friend?" She seemed shocked. I told her that if I, a totally untrained person in the field of medicine, could see her condition was not conducive to caring for a small child, who had just been through this terrible experience, then WHY would the hospital authority release this child to her mother? They, detective Long and Sally of DCF, conferred for a minute and left in quite a rush.

When we got together with the sheriff the next day, he explained why he and Sally had left our house so abruptly. They had not realized that neither the sheriff's office nor DCF had been called by the hospital until the next morning and that was why they had released Andrea to her mother.

CHAPTER SEVEN
"THE INVESTIGATION"

It wasn't long after they left our house, they were in JoAnn's driveway at Island Vista. They wanted to see her and Andrea. A neighbor told them they were at a party, with the baby. The neighbor was asked to contact her and tell her to return home immediately with the child, by order of the Lee County Sheriff's Department.

When she arrived, she was high on the meds again and was over friendly with the sheriff and DCF representative. She seemed to want them to take Andrea and even offered to loan them a car seat from her car. We were led to believe that she had no idea as to what was happening. They took Andrea and she was placed in a temporary shelter for the night. Detective Long told us what they had done the night before, after leaving our place, when we went to have the lie detector test on Sunday afternoon. We were both relieved to hear that, since we were so concerned that Andrea might get hurt again. The lady at the shelter home did call us a couple of days later, to tell us that Andrea was fine and we were welcome and to come visit anytime. She was very kind.

The results of the lie detector tests were that neither Nickie nor I had anything to do with it. Now that this was out of the way, let's concentrate on finding out who molested Andrea.

Lots of things have taken place since that terrible night at the hospital. Andrea is now in the custody of the State of Florida. Since we had asked to get Andrea back home with us, we were thoroughly investigated by DCF and even had a urine test done to make sure neither one of us were using drugs. Even our visiting friend Rosalyn had to be tested also, since she was still with us.

DCF then approved us having custody of Andrea. After staying at the temporary home for about two weeks, we got her back. We were so happy and shed lots of "*happy tears*" together. She had become our reason for living. Eleven days later, we got a call from DCF that a case worker named Stephanie would be at our home to pick up Andrea and take her back to the temporary foster home, where she was before.

We wondered what had happened. It seems that JoAnn had gone to the family court and demanded that Andrea be taken away from us and placed in a temporary foster home again. She indicated that we were the molesters. Even though the lie detector showed that we had nothing to do with this awful crime against our granddaughter, the information was not in the case file. We were not notified of this hearing and since the DCF investigator was out of town, she had sent someone to testify on our behalf. For some reason, the judge did not consider it in rendering his decision regarding where and with whom she would stay.

It was at this time that one of the DCF caseworkers, who wanted to help us, suggested that we hire an attorney to protect our own rights.

The first thing we asked the attorney we had hired was to ask for another hearing before the family judge, since we had not been told about the first one.

Much to our surprise, JoAnn and her friend Eleanor were present. Again, JoAnn repeated her accusation against us. I cannot recall what Eleanor had to say but I do remember we were not too happy with it. We had been advised by our new attorney not to speak and become argumentative in front of the court. She would do all of the talking for us and she was absolutely convinced that we would get Andrea back today. After the judge had heard both sides, he tells the court that he will take this situation under advisement and have a decision no later then 48 hours from now.

The following day we got a call from Sally, the DCF caseworker assigned to our case that the ruling was in and she would e-mail it to us. Much to our surprise, the ruling was that Andrea would be placed in the home of Eleanor and Tim Poore, on the far south side of Ft. Myers. They have a daughter with Down Syndrome which the court believed would be good for Andrea to associate with. It's also suggested that we take this time apart to try and educate ourselves on properly raising a child with DS. Even though we were not happy with the decision of the court, it was obvious that it had been well thought out. The judge gave us unlimited visitation privileges as a way of helping us with the separation. It was still not a happy day for us.

At this time we were told that JoAnn also had visitation with Andrea. She would have to pass a drug test and visits were supervised at the DCF location. I understood this was difficult for her. The day that Andrea was taken to Eleanor's house was not a good day for us. We decided to go out to eat and not mess with cooking and dirty dishes. When we returned, there was a message on our answering machine from Eleanor. She wanted to invite us for supper Sunday evening so we could see where Andrea would be living for the time being.

We called her back and asked if we could have her over the weekend. We had not seen her for a couple weeks and the judge did say that we had unlimited visitation with her. Eleanor was surprised because she had not received a copy of the ruling from the court as yet. Nickie e-mailed it to her, not that she didn't believe us but she would need a copy of this as the foster mom.

When we picked-up Andrea, we arranged the visiting schedule as follow: Friday 8:00 A.M. to Sunday 5:00 P.M. It worked out great and we followed this arrangement for the next few months.

A few weeks later, during a normal physical examination, Andrea's doctor said the tonsils had to be removed NOW. If not, they would cause problems in the future. All arrangements were made and we were told to be at the Health Park Hospital in Ft. Myers at 6:00 A.M. on the morning of the surgery. JoAnn was there also but she decided to wait outside with her girlfriend until it was completed. The attending nurse told us that Andrea was a beautiful little patient and had done real well. I'm not sure if it was a Popsicle or an ice cream bar but Eleanor was allowed to take her home after she had eaten one.

We started to leave and Eleanor asked if we would like to come to her home and spend the rest of the day with Andrea. She felt she would probably need us, when the anesthetic started to wear off. She was right, Andrea hugged me and wouldn't let go until she fell asleep again.

Since I had taken JoAnn's car away from her, which I had paid for, she would not have transportation to show up unexpectedly at Eleanor's house. Yes the car and insurance were in my name. I was told that if ever she would drive home under the influence with a child in the back seat, I could lose Andrea's entire TRUST if she was to hurt or kill someone in an accident and I would be sued for damages.

A Gift from GOD

The day went quite well and I saw a side of Eleanor that I did not know existed. While Nickie was giving Andrea a bath, I found Eleanor with a tear running down her cheek in the kitchen. She told me how ashamed she felt for what she had done to us. She had actually believed all of JoAnn's lies about us and went to court to help her hurt us. She realized now, just how much we really loved this child and hoped that we could forgive her. Six years have passed and we remain friends to this day.

A point of interest: On a Sunday afternoon, we were invited to meet Eleanor, Tim, and their 2 girls and Andrea at a local Rodeo near our house. Sometime during the visit, Tim made a comment that Andrea always referred to us as papa & mama. Tim said: "Only one other time in my life have I heard of a couple being addressed in that way, never was one name mentioned without the other: Tex & AnnaLee." "What did you say?" I said. He repeated it, Tex & AnnaLee. I could hardly believe my ears.

I asked Tim: "Where are you from?" With a certain amount of pride, he said: "Indianapolis, In." Knowing that my uncle Tex lived on Orange Street, on the south side, I asked: "What street did you live on?" He replied: "Orange Street." I asked if this Tex had a big Red REO truck sitting in the back yard with CUSHMAN painted on the door and to his amazement, he said yes. "How did you know that?" he asked me. "Well, get ready for a surprise. The TEX you're referring to was my "UNCLE Tex." He was sort of my mentor as a child and I wanted to be just like him. His wife, Anna Lee didn't really like me." Tim told me that the two families would spend most holidays together, like Thanksgiving, Christmas, etc. He too looked up to my uncle. He was a great man.

Are you a gambler? What do you think the odds are of this happening in a man's lifetime? Here I am, 60 years later, living 1000+ miles from my hometown of Indianapolis, in the state of Florida. I meet a man and his wife Eleanor, who the state has appointed to care for my granddaughter in the absence of her mother, for the next few months, as foster parents. My daughter, her mother had lost her parental rights and we, my wife and I were trying to get guardianship of Andrea for the balance of our lives. The next chapter (#8) will explain how this guardianship application took place and why.

On April 19th, her brother's birthday, JoAnn experienced her first overdose of meds. We, her neighbor and I, found her unconscious laying across her bed. We immediately called 911 and within minutes they arrived and attempted to bring her out of the unconscious state she was in. They decided to transport her to the Cape Coral Hospital and have her stomach pumped. She would spend the night in the hospital under observation and her friend would bring her home the following day. After this experience, she decided to enroll herself into a drug treatment clinic in Naples, Fl., some 50 miles south of Ft. Myers.

What she really wanted to do was show the court that she was trying to get help. Maybe the judge would take this into consideration when deciding if she could again be Andrea's mother, someday. I had my doubts because this judge was far too sharp to be influenced by this.

The treatment center was called "The Willows". A couple weeks later we got a call from them. They wanted to meet the parents and have a face-to-face confrontation, between the 3 of us. We, her mother and I, had been through this some years back at a treatment center in the state of Montana.

The parents would sit in the middle of a circle and all current patients at the clinic, and the user (our daughter in this case), would sit in a circle of about 20 feet in diameter. It was a terrible experience for my wife and me. She beat on us verbally for almost 30 minutes. She talked about things in her life as she was growing up that we had long ago forgotten. It was quite a show and very hurtful. For what? We did all we could to help her through these trying years of growing into adulthood.

We agreed to come to the Willows, only if the face-to-face was conducted in the privacy of one room with JoAnn, Nickie and I, along with the therapist. The confrontation was nothing to write home about, as they say. I asked JoAnn in a very calm voice: "JoAnn, what was it that made you think you could put us through another 8 years of hell, like before? I hope someday you will realize how much your mother and I love you." She just sat there with "glassy" eyes starring right through me. It was almost like they had her on something to get thru any confrontation with us.

So the therapist would understand where I was coming from, I filled in some of the blanks for her: "You see this is the 2nd time we, my wife and I, have been down this road. I had a very lucrative career and a substantial income. So we both got accused of sexual molestation against this daughter and she sued us for 1 MILLION dollars. False Memory Syndrome was the vehicle used to come up with this accusation. We were asked to appear on "ABC Nightline" and given 12 minutes to tell their audience, why this accusation was totally false. Our daughter was given the same 12 minutes to tell her side of things. At one point in her comments she said: "You people watching this, just don't understand. I loved my father. He was bigger than life to me." And this was the same daughter that said I regularly molested her at night, in our basement. The only problem with all this was, we lived in a ranch type home which had NO BASEMENT! So now you know why I am asking the question. The last time we were accused of these falsehoods, we never saw our daughter for 8 years. We love our daughter and granddaughter Andrea, far too much to go through this again."

JoAnn looked at me with eyes filled with love and hurt. I knew she loved me as I loved her. It took all my energy to not break down in tears myself. I knew I would not get an answer and I didn't. We, Nickie and I, left and drove home. We didn't talk much; it had been a draining experience for both of us. Oh how I wished Andrea was home, so I could give her a big hug. You can't imagine how much I needed that.

A couple weeks later, I got a call again from The Willows. It was JoAnn asking me if I would meet her at the Island Vista front gate in an hour, or so. She would not be able to get home with 2 large suitcases by herself. So I was waiting for her when the limo arrived.

I helped her with her things, than started to leave. She asked if I would stay for a few minutes. She wanted to know if I would get her another car. I had to tell her NO because of what happened the night she met with Detective Long in her driveway. She was definitely under the influence and had driven across town with our granddaughter in the back seat.

She started to cry and I so wanted to hold her in my arms but I knew I couldn't. I said to her "Goodbye, I love you." Her reply before I left will be with me until I pass on to my next life: "Dad, do you realize I'm going to die here, in this home, if I have no way to get out and try and rebuild my life?" She had a bicycle and probably 50 established businesses within walking distances. I again told her that I loved her and left.

Less than a week or so passed and we again got a call, this time from the neighbor across the street to tell me that JoAnn had again overdosed and she had been taken to Lee Memorial Hospital in Ft. Myers by ambulance. We were told she will survive, with a few days' rest.

Our attorney then advised us that another hearing had been scheduled at the insistence of the Guardian ad Litem who represented Andrea at 2:00 P.M. on June 7, 2005.

We were at the courthouse a little early and noticed that there were other people waiting for our hearing to start. I was too nervous to see who all were there. The judge had everybody lined up across the front of his bench. He proceeded to ask each person the same question: "Where, in your opinion, does Andrea belong?" All persons, 8 or 9 of them that had been involved in our case, in one way or another, answered: "With her grandparents, Nickie and Jerry Bishop." At that point the judge hit the gavel and said, to Nickie, looking right at her: "She is all yours. Good luck and GOD bless you both."

June 7th, 2005. This was the day I knew that GOD had heard all of my prayers. We were now going to be a real family. No more DRUGS, no more MIND ALTERING MEDICINES and no more sleepless nights, worrying about who was calling us at 3:00 A.M. Tomorrow was going to be the first day of the rest of my life.

CHAPTER EIGHT
"A SPARED LIFE"

This might be a good time to mention the 3 times I cheated death. I knew that GOD had plans for my future life here on earth but I never dreamed that I could be so happy and fulfilled as I am today. I often wondered why my life was spared when it should have been taken.

The first instance was when I was working for Flexco. I had an appointment to work underground at Pyro Mining in West Kentucky, training a crew on the use of belt splices for their conveyors, the following week. When I came home from being out of town all week calling on industrial accounts, I told my wife that I was really tired and needed a change. How about we take next week off and go visit my sister in Florida? Nickie agreed with me and thought it was a wonderful idea. She reminded me of my appointment the following Wednesday night at Pyro Mine.

I called the mine superintendent and asked for a 1-week delay. We drove to Florida to see my sister who lived in North Ft. Myers. It was a great visit with her and her husband. The following night, Thursday to be precise, while watching the evening National News, I saw an aerial view of what appeared to be a Pyro mining property. We increased the volume to hear that a methane gas explosion had killed 11 miners, the night before. The night I was supposed to have been underground with this crew.

I tried to go underground again one more time, during my career at Flexco. When I arrived at the bottom, as it's called, I started hyperventilating and was taken topside immediately. Sometime later I was offered a swap of territories with another salesman. I gave up the coalmines and received in exchange, the St. Louis, Mo. industrial markets. The sales totals were almost an even match so it was a good swap for both of us.

I worked a few more years and decided to retire early at 60 instead of the usual 65. It was not a good move. I was lost without work to do. I did some part time work to keep busy and played a lot of tennis after we moved to Florida.

The second time I cheated death was on a business trip to Grand Rapids, MI. I decided to take my wife Nickie with me and we flew one of our own private planes. All went well until we started the trip back home around noon the following day. The sky was a pretty blue, for as far as the eye could see, so we decided an instrument flight plan would not be necessary. On take off, everything was normal. Then with a big gust of wind, we found ourselves in a summer squall and in what could be serious trouble. I called the control tower and asked for help in keeping us from hitting some radio towers that were at 2500 feet. They had us on radar, so they kept an eye on us and we managed to clear them. I was asked if there was anyone on board that had an instrument rating and I responded that I did, so I gave the controls to Nickie, (who is also a pilot) and I proceeded to prepare an Instrument Flight plan.

After it was done, we were then in the hands of a controller for the rest of the trip home. At this time, I asked if we could be directed out of this weather and was told we were right in the middle and expect to be flying in it for at least 45 minutes or so. The aircraft, a 4 place Piper Archer, started bouncing up and down. It would lose lift and we would drop some 1000 feet. Our heads would hit the roof of the cabin and then we would try and regain our altitude and we would be forced upward and then another drop of 1000 feet. It was horrible...

Nickie and I both saw rivets from the engine cowling pop out but neither of us talked about it. We knew this would probably kill us before we got out of the squall. "Highways in the Sky" being on a flight plan, required that we fly in a 1 mile wide corridor. The controller kept telling us we were outside of this and had to get back on track. At this point, I told her that we were doing all that was possible to just stay right side up and for them to watch our direction because we had our hands full as it was. She agreed and then... we saw what appeared to be a glimmer of sunshine off in the distance. It was like GOD sending us a message that said: "You are almost home." It had been the better part of 2 hours fighting this battle to stay alive but with God's help we made it.

When we landed in Fishers, Indiana, we asked the gasman if they had had a storm in the last few hours. He looked up towards Heaven and said: "What you see is what you get. It's been a beautiful day." Then he said, "How's your day been?" We only smiled back at him.

On our drive back home, we admitted to each other that we had seen lightning and knowing how dangerous lightning can be if it strikes the airplane, neither one of us had mentioned it to the other. We both thanked the LORD in our own way and headed home to be with the children we love.

The third time was quite a bit less eventful. Later on, we had a Piper Saratoga, 6 place aircraft with a 3 bladed propeller and retractable landing gear. It was quite fast with a cruising speed of sometimes 200 knots or more per hour. One night coming home from a trip, we entered the pattern to land. Our speed was tapering off but suddenly I saw that I was about to hit the plane in front of us. It was a small 2 place trainer type aircraft cruising along at about 80 knots or so. I immediately upped the land gear and made a hard right, to miss his rudder, by maybe 10 feet at the most. Had the landing gear been down and locked, I'm sure I would not be sitting here writing this.

Like I wrote before, GOD had a plan for Nickie and I and her name was Andrea.

CHAPTER NINE
"THE FATAL CALL"

It's very difficult to try and explain what we had been thru these last few months. Everyday was adventuress, to say the least. We felt we really needed to get away for a few days. Our first stop was Indianapolis, In. where we picked up our granddaughter Sadie that would accompany us to Canada. We decided to drive and just enjoy the trip. After about a week there, we drove to Montreal, Canada. Most of Nickie's family had never seen Andrea, so it was a good visit for all.

During the trip we received 2 telephone calls from JoAnn. The first, she was not too happy. She asked her mother: "What do you mean taking my daughter on vacation without telling me?" Her mother reminded her that she had not asked to see Andrea for the last month or so and she had to have known that the judge had given us full custody, so we didn't think we needed her approval.

Once in Indiana, I received another call from her. She wanted me to call her when we arrived in Montreal, Canada. She indicated she was concerned as to our safety. Once we arrived, we suddenly became so busy with relatives, I forgot all about returning her call. I regretted this later.

We visited for about 5 days. It was great seeing everybody fussing over Andrea. She was definitely the hit of the party. We left Thursday of that week for the trip home. Shortly after leaving my mother-in-law's home, Andrea started crying, actually sobbing uncontrollably – what's wrong? This child seldom ever cried, only when she was physically hurt. We kept asking her if she was hurting anywhere and she kept shaking her head "NO" and kept crying. Nickie finally told our granddaughter Sadie that was sitting next to her in the back seat, to take Andrea out of her car seat and hold her for a little while. Sadie did as requested, held Andrea and kept talking soothingly to her. She finally calmed down, stopped crying and gave us a big smile. Both Nickie and I were puzzled by what had just taken place...

Usually when visiting Canada, we always traveled on Hwy 401, which is a super highway that stretches from Detroit/Windsor to Montreal, 600 miles of super multi lanes of boring highway. To enjoy our return trip this time, we re-entered the USA through New York. We would be bypassing Indiana and basically following the east coast to Florida. It was a much more beautiful trip than the boring highway I mentioned before.

We arrived home, in N. Fort Myers, Fl. late Friday night. All very tired but nothing a good night's sleep couldn't correct. The following day, we received a call from JoAnn's minister. He had received a call from her friend Mike, who was then working out of state. For the past couple days, he had called her and left word for her to return his call. She had not which was not like her. She always called him back within a couple of hours. He called their church to have someone check on her. The assistant minister found nothing out of the ordinary on the property so they called us to check the inside of the home and also to find out if we had talked to her in the last few days. We told him no because we had just returned from Canada the night before.

At this point, we asked Margaret her next door friend and neighbor to see if JoAnn was okay. She went over, checked the house and found nothing suspicious either except when she looked into the front door window, which allowed her to see the kitchen table. JoAnn's purse was sitting there, indicating something was wrong because this was a person that went absolutely nowhere without her purse. After Margaret called us, I called the Lee County Sheriff's Department dispatcher knowing something had to be wrong.

I explained to the dispatcher what had been happening in the past few weeks. I suspected another overdose of medication and I simply could not go thru this again, finding her in that state. Would they please check on my daughter for me? They understood what we had been going through and it was not a problem. Arrangements were made for me to meet the officer in front of the house with a key to the front door. He would then enter to check that things were okay. He arrived and I told him that I really appreciated his help because I had found JoAnn unconscious from overdoses twice before and I just could not do it again.

I stood at the end of the driveway while he entered the house. He was inside a very short time and when he came out he lowered his head and said: "I'm sorry Mr. Bishop but your daughter is dead!" YES, JoAnn's pain and suffering had come to an end. Being in shock, as her father, I shed no tears at the time. I knew she was with our LORD and for this I was GRATEFUL.

I stayed at the house until all was taken care of by the sheriff's department. The city morgue was called to come take our daughter's body downtown. After the house was all checked out, the officer returned the key to me. I locked up and headed home to be with Nickie.

JoAnn

As I left I called her on my cell phone and asked that she take Andrea next door to June's house for the next couple hours or so. Even though Nickie and I were not really surprised that this had happened, we kept praying and hoping that it wouldn't. One night, a few weeks earlier, Nickie and I had gotten down on our knees and prayed to God to help our daughter to let go of her addiction and start a new life. I'm sure she knew how much we loved her and would have done anything to help her but she first had to help herself. Obviously, the addiction to drugs was more powerful than anything else.

We were both in shock but being the "DOER" that I am, I proceeded to call our family and friends, while Nickie just sat in the kitchen crying and did not want to talk to anyone. I asked our son if he wanted me to tell his daughter Sadie and he told me no, that he preferred to tell her himself. Since he needed time to compose himself, he told me that he would call back in an hour. Sadie really loved her aunt JoAnn and was very saddened by the news. I also called Christopher's father and he assured us that as soon as he found out what the arrangements were, he would send his son to attend his mother's funeral.

The officer that found her had told me there was no note, only an empty bottle that had contained 90 capsules of muscle relaxants. It was assumed that these had been taken some 48 hours before she was found. The death certificate was dated Saturday, June 25, 2005 as the time of death.

Point of interest: Once we found out that she had probably died a couple of days earlier, Nickie and I looked at each other and had the same thought: this would have been on Thursday... could this have been the reason why Andrea had cried that morning in the car? Was this when JoAnn died and her soul left her body? Did Andrea feel it and without understanding why, she experienced a great sadness at losing her mother? Of course, we will not find the answer to this question until we get to heaven ourselves but as long as we live, we choose to believe that this is what happened.

Nickie and I both wanted to remember our daughter JoAnn as she was in life, so we did not identify the body. This was done from photos and other forms of identification. She was cremated a few days later.

Our good friend Rosalyn

Rosalyn, a good friend of ours from Indiana, also flew in. She and our daughter Lynn, who lives in Bushnell, FL., spent a couple days going through old photo albums and created 2 large posters depicting JoAnn's life. These were displayed on the altar at the memorial service held at a Christian Church in Cape Coral, Fl. on July 3, 2005. JoAnn's son, Christopher, her sister Lynn and her brother Bryan were all in attendance at the service. It was held at the last church that JoAnn had attended in the area. Her daughter Andrea being only 4 years of age at the time of her death, did not really comprehend what had happened, so we felt it would be better if she did not attend the service.

Following the service, the family and Rosalyn went to a favorite place of JoAnn's, along the Caloosahatchee River where we sprinkled some of her ashes. She used to go there often to sit and watch the sunsets with Andrea. At that time, our son Bryan asked if he could have some of the ashes to take home to Indiana. The following year, he bought a cemetery plot and tombstone, where he buried her ashes. Since Bryan took the death of his sister very hard, it was important for him that on the first anniversary of her death, he would have a memorial service that would be attended by family and friends that could not be in Florida the year before.

Andrea & Rosalyn

A couple of months after JoAnn's passing, Andrea asked her grandmother to go to her mommy's house. Nickie explained to her that her mommy had gone to heaven to be with Jesus. That seemed to satisfy her and she accepted it.

In November of the same year, we went to Indiana to be with our family for Thanksgiving. It was to be Andrea's first flight in an airplane. We made sure she had a window seat so that she could see everything outside. Two months later she was pulling a little suitcase toward the front door, I asked: "Where are you going?" She answered: "I'm going to the airport to catch a plane. Then I'm going to see my mommy in heaven." I told her to have a safe trip. She pretended to open the door, turned around and went back to her bedroom. We were amazed at her understanding and acceptance at the loss of her mother. We could see that she remembered our flight to Indiana and the plane ascending in the sky up towards heaven and she decided to fly there to see her mommy. What an insight for a four-year-old child.

She of course attended the Memorial Service in June of the following year. By then she was aware of her Mother's passing and had accepted it. She was now better prepared to attend with the family.

Christopher

After the service in Cape Coral, **Christopher** (JoAnn' son) was to return to Oklahoma where he lived with his father. But before leaving, he wanted to ask his Grandmother a question: "Did my mother take too many pills by accident or did she do it on purpose?" I recall Nickie saying: "I don't really know for sure Chris! As you know, your mother was a very sick person and she took a lot of medicine for pain. A prescription bottle was found in bed with her that was totally empty of 90 muscle relaxant pills. This prescription had been filled only 2 days earlier. So this would suggest that maybe she was in such severe pain that she took the entire bottle during a short period of time. Since the HEART is a muscle and if she took that many relaxants at one time, it could have relaxed the heart to the point of stopping it. Like I said, I really don't know whether it was accidental or not and I guess we will never know for sure. Just remember, she loved both you and Andrea very much."

Christopher boarded the plane and he is now back in Oklahoma with his dad. At this writing, he has one week before he leaves for boot camp in the U.S. Navy. As previously mentioned, he will apply for the SEALS after his basic training is completed, which should take somewhere around 9 weeks. This last summer, he has been working with a body trainer so he should be in great shape. He is a fine young man and I feel he will be a good addition to the SEAL organization.

A point of interest: After the memorial service, Detective Long called to tell us that he was closing the investigation. They had talked with her friend from Washington that was visiting her at the time, had interviewed most of her neighbors and friends and had never been able to determine who had molested Andrea. Consequently, knowing that Andrea was now safe in our care and since JoAnn had passed away, they had decided to terminate the investigation.

Rosalyn stayed over after the Memorial service. She and I cleaned JoAnn's home and got it ready for sale. One thing Nickie and I did not need was another house payment, so we hoped it would sell quickly. We had everything in our name, anticipating something like this could possibly happen and we wanted no legal entanglements, when it was necessary to sell the house and payoff the loan.

Cleaning a house this small, where the main resident was a heavy smoker was not an easy task. Of course being a new home, the walls had little paint on them. It didn't take long to realize the walls would basically have to be stripped and repainted with probably 2 or 3 coats of fresh paint. John and Margaret, the next door neighbors agreed to take on this project for a fee and they did a really great job. Not only did they paint all the walls, they did a lot of the wood trim and the place looked like a brand new unit, when they were done. Since my mother, Grandma Kay, had lost her home to hurricane Charlie the previous year, most of her furniture was used to re-decorate JoAnn's house before it was put up for sale. It fit really well and made the home look really nice.

We gave the sales contract to the park property manager and she did a great job of selling the house in the first 30 days of the listing. The bank in Noblesville, In. where we had secured the loan was very pleased to receive a check for the full unpaid balance on the loan.

It was good to have everything that needed done completed in the first 45 days after JoAnn's passing. I feel sure she is with Jesus and all the pain she lived with has left her. I miss her but I am happy for her at the same time.

In the days following her passing, we discovered that she had talked to many of her friends and family members about the care of Andrea. She said she knew that her Mom and Dad would take good care of her because they loved her so very much. Yes, we do love her and now is the time to get on with the task of raising her properly.

CHAPTER TEN
"A NEW CHAPTER OF OUR LIVES"

It's already early July and time to get Andrea enrolled into a good pre-K school class. She was now walking pretty good unlike last year when she had a metal walker. The school had wanted us to have her start the year before but she was not walking and we wanted no part of a wheelchair for her. She had a great year and seemed to just love going to school and being with the other children.

Andrea was still quite small at this time. We heard lots of comments like: "Surely that little girl is not going to school yet!" Like I mentioned before, her book bag covered over half of her body since she was so tiny.

It was great to see her starting to grasp and learn things that would be a part of her future. It became very obvious that the teacher and her 2 assistants really cared for Andrea and made sure when she was on the playground that she was looked after and protected from any danger.

At the beginning of the year, she had fallen twice and had bloody knees when I picked her up in the afternoon. Remember that she had not been walking for very long and was not running like the other kids her age. Being a protective grandpa as I am, I made sure the school provided an assistant to be with her while playing on the cement slab, which they called the playground. She never fell again and I believe the assistant enjoyed the time as much as Andrea did.

A few months earlier, I think around February or so, Andrea was taken to the Special Equestrians ranch by her foster mother Eleanor. We of course were called and asked to meet her there. It was a wonderful thing to see all of these "special needs" children on their selected horses. Some we were told could not walk, stand up or have any mobility to speak of and now they were sitting in the saddle of a real live horse and appeared to be totally in control of the situation.

Andrea as a young rider

Somehow they found a little horse for Andrea, since she was so small. Its name was **KING** and he was a 30 year old horse, which was not a pony but not a full size horse either. Andrea and King became good friends during the following 5 years or so. She even learned to ride King while standing upright. When she had a growth spurt, this relationship came to an abrupt end. She grew about 12 inches and gained some 25 lbs in one summer and this was just too much load for this little horse. So, she now rides a full size horse named Scarlet. She is just about ready to begin riding without side walkers. Bill Curtis, her trainer for the last 6 years, is not happy about leaving her side. He has been her side walker since she started almost 7 years ago. They had developed quite a relationship and will be friends for many years to come I'm sure. This change of horses for Andrea happened just a few weeks ago and I could see the disappointment in Bill's eyes. He told me, with tears in his eyes, that he would no longer be working with Andrea after all this time. He loves her so much as she loves him also.

Next he did something that I think describes what Bill C. is all about. He took Andrea, Nickie and I aside where he was not overheard, to tell us that he was needed by a little boy that had almost drowned. He was under water for some time and had lost all functions of a 3 year old. These would have to be rebuilt and he had been asked to help with the process. He told Andrea he loved her but she had been such a good student that she didn't need him beside her anymore. Soon she would be riding alone in total control of Scarlet's movements.

She accepted this better than me because I knew how much he loved this little girl. This is the child he had helped to develop into who she is today. Three years ago, she had been awarded the trophy for being the "Rider of the Year" for Special Equestrians of Lee County, Florida. She is truly a champion in her own right. So there she is on this big horse, our little Andrea sitting up there knowing what she is doing and doing it well. We are so proud of her.

Let me share with you a little bit about who these volunteer people are and what they are all about. Bill has been with Special Equestrians for the past 23 years. He is like a part of our family. He and his girlfriend Gina often take Andrea to live shows at the Barbara Mann Theater in Ft. Myers, FL. Recent shows that she has seen are: Aladdin, Cat in a Hat, Annie and the Rockettes and others. Dinner is served before some of the shows begin and Andrea just loves going with them.

It might be interesting to know that Andrea has only been allowed to be with 3 other people in her short life. She calls her time with Bill and Gina her special dates. We trust them as we do the others but I don't mind telling you that I am a nervous wreck until she rings the doorbell arriving home again.

I recall reading somewhere that children with Down Syndrome are the most often "special needs" children to be kidnapped in America. I see what is going on in our society today with children being abused and it just makes me sick. I don't know what I would do if Andrea was ever taken from me. I have a love for her, like I do for my wife of 52 years but, it's a different kind of love. I really do not know how to describe it. The best way is to say, it's a relationship between a big person and a little person that is very special to both of us. She is my "*honey bun*" and I am her "*lover dover*" (her description).

I wake up most mornings with a smile because I am about to see Andrea after a long night's sleep.

She'll start my day with: "Good morning PaPa!" and usually that comes with a big hug and a big smile. She is now in her 2nd year of Pre-K because of her size. We felt she needed to be a little bit bigger to be with the other children that were to be in Kindergarten.

Special needs children have what is called an ESE meeting twice a year or more, if the parent of such child feels a need for a special meeting to discuss issues of concern to them. The ESE stands for "Exceptional Student Education." This is a state run organization, as in our case under The School District of Lee County, Florida. Persons associated with this organization are exceptional people with only the child's best interest in mind. It's good to know there is someone looking out for your child other than just you, as you will see later in this chapter.

Andrea is doing well at school. She is sort of the favorite of all that have met her. We also decided to enroll her into a dancing school so she could meet other young girls in her age group. The first year she took ballet. She tried so hard but it was obvious that she had Downs and was not as agile as the others. Of course we knew she had low muscle tone but the idea of dancing school was to help with improving this situation, just as the horseback riding and swimming have done for her.

All 3 of these activities have been very good for Andrea's social life and she has made a lot of friends over the years. As I am writing this, she is in her sixth year of dancing and seventh year of horseback riding.

During this time period, Rosalyn was living with us. She and Andrea were sharing a room together. She and Nickie had taught Andrea to swim while we lived at Tara Woods before moving into our new home. Have you heard the term, "*took to it like fish to water*". Well Andrea did. I'll tell you more about this later in this chapter.

For the past year or so we had been having a new home built. We wanted Andrea and Grandma "Kay" to have their own rooms and closets. Building a home in Florida was something to see. You had to see it because no sane person would believe it. It seemed that every time a nail was driven into a piece of wood, everything STOPPED. An inspection had to be done! Is this what they call creative employment or what? Our new home was 2500+ square feet, on a slab of concrete, with a 2 car attached garage and a pool that measured 28'x14'. It took 18+ months to build from start to finish. The workmanship was beyond reproach and they did a good job, even though it took a year and a half.

As mentioned, Andrea was swimming laps of 28 feet round trip 4 to 5 times per day, once we moved into our new home. She was like a little fish. To assure that she would be able to work with this daily therapy, regardless of weather, we installed 2 pool heaters. One being an electric heat pump and the other less costly was a solar system with 9 panels. The initial cost was more for the latter, but over the long run it worked out to be of less cost then the monthly electric bill increase during the colder months of winter.

You know when you have a house built, all the walls are generally an off white color so we painted Andrea's room lavender with pink window coverings. She was thrilled with it. Next was the new furniture for her, all white enamel with a trundle bed. Why? I do not know. Andrea is not allowed to have sleepovers so this bed is used mostly for overnight company. When our three children became adults, all of them without exception, explained to us how they were introduced to the "*good life*" as they called it back then. Drugs, alcohol, sexual experimentation or anything else they knew they could not do at home. It is my belief that when you allow your children to sleep over with friends, you give up your parental authority to another adult that probably doesn't love your child as you do.

We have had father daughter talks on this subject and Andrea seems to grasp what I am talking about. She has a habit of thinking about something such as this and maybe 10 to 15 minutes later, she will come to me and say: "You are right PaPa. I will sleep in my own bed, it's a good idea."

I don't know whether this has to do with having Down Syndrome or not, but we find her to be extremely cooperative in most situations. A recent example that just happened this morning at breakfast, I had bought her two doughnuts. One iced with chocolate and the other with orange icing. She ate the first and wanted another. I said no because I know that this is the time when they have a tendency to blossom out and gain a lot of weight, if you don't control their eating habits. Again, she agreed with me. She came, stood in front of me, extended her arms for a hug and said: "PaPa, you are so smart and I love you so very much." I recall that she did eat it later in the day, after she digested the first one!

I have to be one of the luckiest men on the face of the earth, to have such an understanding child to raise and to love.

CHAPTER ELEVEN
"A MIRACLE CALLED ANDREA"

Andrea, age 6

Andrea is now in a regular 1st grade class and having some problems keeping up. We received a call from the ESE Department that a meeting had been called and we were requested to be there. Her teacher and all of the therapists that provided services to her were present and they were all given an opportunity to state their feelings regarding Andrea's education.

First off, the class size was something in the neighborhood of between 25 and 27 students, one teacher with no assistants. Andrea was lucky to get a good morning, let alone any individual attention that was needed to properly educate her.

At the ESE meeting the previous year, it had been decided to place her in a regular 1st grade class, since she had done well in kindergarten. She had done well this time too until after the holidays. Then she started to regress a bit and the ESE people brought it to our attention.

Andrea was then transferred to Littleton Elementary and was placed in a class along with one teacher with two assistants and nine other students. There were actually three different grade levels in this one classroom and a really wonderful teacher named Ms. Bronson. We saw a big improvement from Andrea and her attitude regarding school, which was immediately noticeable. She really liked Ms. Bronson and her assistants.

Early in the year, our good friend Rosalyn's future daughter-in-law Stacy, from Indiana, called Andrea and asked if she would be the flower girl at her and Clay's wedding in July. The wedding was outside in a small park and all went very well. The reception was in an adjoining open air structure and we all had a really great time. Andrea was dancing with one of Rosalyn's grandsons Daylen, the ring bearer and they both seemed to be really enjoying themselves, as the photos will show.

As you have probably noticed, there is a splattering of photos throughout the book, which I hope you are enjoying. For example, here is a photo of **Daylen and Andrea** dancing together. Notice the look of pride on her face.

Andrea & Daylen at wedding

That same year, on December 10, 2008 to be exact, we received a call from Michele, Nickie's sister from Canada, to inform us that her mother had passed away during the night. She was almost 99 years old. We found out a couple of days later that the funeral would take place the following weekend since so many people were coming from out of town and had to make reservations, arrangements, etc. We decided that since there would only be a few days of school left before the Christmas holidays, Nickie would take Andrea with her. The last time Andrea had visited Nickie's family had been in June 2005, so most people found that she had grown and matured quite a bit.

We had explained to her that **Grandma Marcoux,** she referred to her as "*Grandma Coucou*", had gone to heaven to be with her mommy and she took it very well. They stayed in her mom's apartment, which was close to her sister's and brother's place. Andrea promptly discovered a stuffed cat that she decided to call "*Snowflake*" since it was all white. They asked her sister if she could take it home and of course Michele said yes, she was welcome to take her great grandma's cat. She has been sleeping with it ever since.

Nickie's mother

At the funeral, Nickie got to see a lot of her relatives that she had not seen for a long time. Many of them met Andrea for the first time and were amazed at how well behaved she was. Nickie had explained to her that during the funeral service in the chapel, she had to be very quiet and when she went up front to talk (to pay tribute to her Mom), she had to stay with her aunt Michele and remain quiet. She did and when Nickie went back to the pew and sat down next to her and was crying, she wiped her tears away. A lot of people sitting around them noticed what she was doing and commented later, on how sweet and loving they thought she was.

Andrea & Michele

The day of the funeral was a beautiful cold but clear day. The next day, there was a snowstorm so Nickie and Andrea stayed in and rested. On Monday, her sister Michele picked them up and took them to her house. Since we live in Florida, Andrea had never seen this much snow. Michele and she went out to play in it and make angels. Nickie stayed in the house and took pictures of them thru the front window. Andrea said she really enjoyed playing in the snow but was happy to come in and take off those snowy clothes and warm up with a cup of hot chocolate. She later told us that even though she enjoyed playing in the snow for a while, she preferred living in Florida where it is warm most of the time.

A cold day in Canada

May 28, 2009. Today is Andrea's 8th birthday party. I went to the Target Bakery this morning to pick up the cake of Hanna Montana design. She will be so happy seeing all of her friends, mostly adults and I know she will have a wonderful day.

School is going along just fine. Ms. Bronson is doing a great job with her. She will be going on a cruise during spring break as a reward for her efforts and hard work. That's a deal I made with her. If she passes her semester and advances to the next higher grade level, she is rewarded with a 7 day cruise on a Carnival Cruise Ship. They are very organized and have scheduled programs for all children on board. It's like being in play school but a whole lot more fun. Plus it gives the parents some time alone to go shopping or do whatever.

This cruise idea was a way to reward not only Andrea but to also reward us. We, throughout our married life, have always enjoyed cruising and I would believe we have gone on more than 15 cruises during the last 30 years or so.

There is a draw back though. For those of you that have been on a cruise, you know what I mean, right? You seem to be eating almost continuously. I can still remember our first cruise, the ship was named the "*Mardi Gras*", a rather small vessel by today's standards but definitely a "FUN" ship as they are referred to. In talking to the crewmembers, we discovered that she was to be decommissioned and refurbished after this final cruise, probably re-named and sold to one of the smaller cruise lines.

Andrea really enjoyed her first cruise. She was the perfect little passenger. She slept with Nickie and when it was time for bed, she would turn away from the light and within 10 minutes she was fast asleep. No arguments at all. She seems to know when she has had a full day and is tired. She is such a wonderful child. I feel so sorry for those persons that feel it is a burden for Nickie and I to have such a child. You know, I believe that GOD made only a few children with Down Syndrome. He knew how special they were to be and to whom he would entrust their futures to.

CHAPTER TWELVE
"GOD'S MYSTERIOUS WAYS"

In chapter eight, I shared with you the three times I actually felt that I had cheated death. It's interesting to note that all three instances occurred before Andrea was conceived in her mother's womb. I used to wonder why had GOD let me live when I should have died with those guys in the coalmine? The other two times, I was again saved for some unknown purpose. It took Andrea to teach me that God did have a purpose for my life and it was to be here when she needed us to be her Mommy and PaPa, when her mother JoAnn was called to Heaven.

Here I was, 65 years of age, retired for the past five years. I had recently been cheated out of almost $800,000 by my financial planner, who was not the person he professed to be. And if this wasn't enough, a daughter who had recently overdosed on pain medicine and died, leaving her four year old daughter with Down Syndrome and no mommy and daddy. Then the State of Florida placed Andrea in a foster home for four months, while they investigated Nickie and I for whatever. We had a lie detector test, FBI checks and our neighbors were questioned as to what kind of people we were.

Thank goodness I still had Nickie, my wife of 52 years. It seemed as though everyday of our life was some sort of an event. Remember that TV show, "behind Curtain #1 #2 or #3." Well, for a couple of years it seemed as though we never knew what was coming our way next.

Now, let's fast forward a few years and see how things are going.

Andrea is in school, leaving on the bus at 6:20 A.M. and returning around 3:20 P.M. everyday doing quite well.

Nickie is the property manager for a Canadian firm that presently owns three rental properties in South West, FL. She probably works about 15 to 20 hours per week, cleaning, accounting and other duties like paying taxes, etc.

I am working for a wholesale food distribution company, in N. Ft. Myers, FL. calling on restaurants in the area for food sales. My job responsibilities are to call on establishments that have never bought food before from our company. I ask for a menu from which a quotation is prepared in order to give the prospective customer an opportunity to check out our prices. If food samples are requested, I supply them also.

We have a good routine with Andrea. Mondays are dance classes at Dance Dimension Studio. Tuesdays are Special Equestrians and on our weekends, we look forward to having a breakfast date every other week, just Andrea and I. It is a special time to have our Father-Daughter talks that we both enjoy tremendously. Nickie and Andrea swim every chance they get, weather permitting.

Most Saturdays Nickie and I check out the 3 rental properties to make sure all is O.K. We also check that the alarm is on and working properly. Sometimes Andrea comes with us but most times she wants to stay home with her Grandma Kay and play games and such. They have a good relationship and it's important that she has this time with her alone.

As you can see, we have a pretty full life with Andrea and Grandma Kay being a part of it. One other thing I have failed to mention is that Grandma Kay does all the cooking and baking, which is something she enjoys doing. This gives Nickie and me the opportunity to earn a little extra income. It doesn't make up for the $800K loss but it gives us a little extra money to provide for Andrea. We try not to spoil her but we realize and we are very grateful to be able to provide these extras that most little girls her age would enjoy. My intention is to continue working as long as I am capable to do so.

Our son, Bryan called me a few months back and said, he had been thinking about Andrea and us for the last few days and had something he felt needed to be said at this time. He wanted Nickie and me to know that Andrea would never be left without a home. When our time comes to join JoAnn in the after life, she would become the 3rd child in his home. I think he knows just how much pressure was relieved from us with this telephone call. If not, he will read it here when this book is published. We say: "Thank You" to our dear son, Bryan.

CHAPTER THIRTEEN
"LIFE AS IT STANDS"

In February of 2011, we were again invited to an ESE meeting, to talk about Andrea's further education in the Lee County School System. All agreed that she had made excellent progress at Littleton Elementary but now was the time to put her into a class especially designed for "Special Needs" children called "Life Skills". This is where the student is taught how to live on their own as they grow into adulthood. A lot of what they are taught the first year, Andrea already knew to the surprise of her teacher: like drying dishes, dusting furniture, making beds, dressing herself and taking care of her personal hygiene. We were told also that later she will be taught to ride a bus alone, write a resume and interview for a job; how to shop and pay for groceries and balance a checkbook. It is decided that she will attend Hancock Creek Elementary School where such a class is available. She will be on the bus about 2½ hours per day but she doesn't seem to mind it. When tired, she will take a nap and the driver's assistant will awake her when she gets home.

So far this year, we have visited the teacher on two occasions. She tells us that Andrea is a very good student and is always there to help with the clean-up at the end of the day. She gets along well with her fellow students and is loved by all the school staff.

It's April 23rd, Spring Break for Andrea. We are all packed and ready to go on our annual Cruise. This time we are leaving from Miami, FL., so we will drive across Alligator Alley. It's a dull drive with nothing to see but green brush all the way. Thank goodness we have TV in the van so she can play her games along the way. I wonder when we get to Miami, will we get lost again? We usually do; this place called Port of Miami is not always easy to find. When we arrive though, the parking is great. You drop off your luggage, drive across the street to a high rise parking garage, then I walk back across the street to meet Nickie and Andrea. Then we, along with a few hundred other passengers, get in line to board the ship after paperwork is completed. Each passenger is given a Credit Card with all pertinent information and then we are ready to go to our cabin and wait for our luggage to arrive. It's a process that we do each time we go on a cruise and it's not really bad. It gives you a chance to meet and talk to others waiting in line with you.

2011 Cruise

The first night at sea, we went to the main dining room for the 6:00 P.M. setting and no one showed up at our table for 12 other then the 3 of us. There seemed to be some mix up with the table assignments and we were told that tomorrow evening there would be two families joining us with their 4 children. Andrea was excited about that.

The following night, as a matter of act, there were two more families with children at our table and it made the cruise so much more enjoyable. As usual, we all had a great time and Andrea is already talking about next year's cruise!

It's now June 10th, 2011. School is completed for Andrea at Littleton Elementary and she says her goodbyes to all of the good teachers and friends she has made. She is looking forward to the change of schools for next semester, beginning August 8th. To her, moving on to a new school, meeting new teachers and friends, is an adventure. She is not sad but excited by the whole experience.

It's great having her home for a few days. I will continue working through out the summer but I will often come by for lunch with my little "*Honey Bun*" whenever working in the area. She has a busy schedule for the next few days. Vacation Bible School begins the 18th and she will have dance rehearsal two nights this week. The actual dance recital will be Saturday, June 18th. The dancers have all worked very hard this season and it should be quite a show. We are looking forward to it.

Gee, the week just flew by. Here we are at the dance recital waiting for the opening curtain at 5:30 P.M. The theme this year is "*A Night at the Oscars*" featuring "*The Wizard of OZ Matinee*". There will be 58 acts featuring all the students of Dance Dimensions Studio.

You would actually have to see this to fully appreciate the amount of work that went in to making this possible. There are little children all dressed in their costumes doing their numbers of song and dance and they are just beautiful. I wanted to jump on the stage and give them all a hug. More than once during these performances, I had to wipe away a tear or two. I guess that comes with old age but I was so moved by the obvious effort these little children had given to entertain their parents and relatives.

Andrea was in the 33rd act called "*Can You Feel the Love Tonight*" which was up for Best Musical. She was so wonderful, I actually cried as I watched her trying to keep up with the other performers. Although the audience may have seen only the DS in her, what we her grandparents saw was our little Andrea trying as best as she could to make us proud of her.

During the summer, Andrea has her annual check-up and as usual, she is in great shape. A lot of children born with Down Syndrome are born with a hole in their heart but thank God, Andrea did not have that problem and has always had a very strong heart. She is also what they call a very "high functioning" child with DS. On the other hand, she has some of the same characteristics that most children with DS have, which are being loving and affectionate.

We're now in the Fall of 2011. Andrea is now 10 years of age and growing faster than a weed. Just in the last few months, she grew about 6 inches in height and put on an additional 15 pounds or so. Not the fatty kind either. These were pounds she needed to fill her out a bit. She has a real cute figure and you would think she is much older than her age.

In raising Andrea, Nickie and I have certain things we each do. This is sort of my responsibility. One of my jobs is to get her up in the morning at 5:45 A.M. and get her ready for school. This used to involve helping her to dress until she started growing into a young lady, if you get my meaning. She couldn't understand why her PaPa could not continue to help her in the morning when this happened. So Nickie took her shopping and got her some training bras and then spent a few mornings getting her used to putting it on correctly. Believe me she put the bra on backwards more than once. Nickie would come to the rescue and when all was right, I would take her in the bathroom, brush her hair and put a color coordinated hair band to match what she was wearing that day. We would then head to the garage to wait for the bus. She always looks so pretty in the morning.

This is where Andrea shows me new dance steps she has seen on TV and she will usually sing a couple songs for me. The driveway is like her own private stage. We have a lot of fun while waiting. We also work on her spelling words. Each week her class is given 10 new words to learn and spell by the end of the week; a test is then given on Friday morning.

I myself was never an 'A' student and for this I am not ashamed. I recall being asked to the Dean's office when in High School as an 11th grader. When I arrived, I was surprised to see my business teacher, waiting for my arrival also. Was I ever confused; I could not recall anything I had done that would warrant such a meeting. You won't believe what happened next. The Dean said: "Jerry, we would like for you to do something for good old Manual High School before you leave us next year."

Remember, I'm just a pimple faced teenager of 17 and this man who is in charge of all school discipline, is asking me to do something for my school! I'm wondering if someone is playing a trick on me or am I losing my mind? Well, what he said next will explain it all. At that point with my chest all puffed out I said: "Mr. Dean, I would be happy to do whatever I can before I graduate if it will make my school a better place for the new students to attend."

Here goes: "Jerry we would like you to promise us that you will not sign up for geometry again. It would be your fourth semester and we feel your presence in a class of freshmen is distracting, considering the fact that you have failed the class three times before." At this point, Jay Ray stood up and said: "Jerry, I have been your business teacher for the past three years and I can tell you, you are never going to design a bridge or build a tall sky scraper. It's just not who you are. But before getting back to class, I will tell you that you will probably end up being the #1 salesman for a large corporation some day. In your senior year, I want to encourage you to take business math instead of geometry, which you obviously cannot master." The following year I did as asked. I got my first and only "A" in 4 years of High School by taking business math as suggested. I felt really good about finding my real calling for adulthood.

I did in fact, after 4 years of military service, end up working for a major corporation located in

Downers Grove, Illinois. They manufactured and distributed conveyor belt fasteners and related products, worldwide. And **it's a big AND**, I did become the #1 salesman as Jay Ray had predicted in 1957. I even received sales award certificates after I had retired. My former sales manager sent me a couple of them for having sold the most belt cleaners of a type, with a nice note. It said: "Even retired, you're still getting sales awards for the fine job of selling, while you were here."

This is how I feel about Andrea also. She too won't design bridges or build large tall buildings or anything like that. But she will be a good person to know and love. Being a goal oriented person as I am, I sat down with Andrea and explained to her what a goal was. You do good and you get a reward or you do bad and you get nothing! Then I added the Dairy Queen to it. "You do good by getting a score of 70% or better on your spelling test and we go to the D.Q. for an ice cream treat on Friday evening." Then I asked her: "What if you get a score of less then 70% . . . say 50% or 60%? What happens then?" "I stay home and get no ice cream!" she said. Andrea, this year so far, has gotten a score of 80% as her lowest, all others have been 90% and 100%.

When you read about my success in becoming the #1 salesman at Flexco, did you wonder why? Well, it certainly wasn't my scholastic achievements, right? It was just a simple 4 letter word "GOAL" that sort of molded my life as I grew into adulthood. I successfully developed a systematic way of setting and achieving goals. It's worked for me as long as I can remember.

I'm hoping to help Andrea in the art of setting and achieving her goals in life also. This I believe will be the greatest gift I can leave her.

EPILOGUE

Before finishing this book, my first attempt as such, there is something I'd like to share with you about Andrea and how she reacted to an emergency during our cruise in April. One morning, she and I decided to go to breakfast together and to let Mommy sleep in. As I have mentioned before, we do this every other weekend when at home. While waiting for the elevator, an older man approached me to ask if I knew where he could find the doctor's office. As it happened, I had been there the night before, getting some cough syrup for Andrea.

I turned around to give him directions and when I turned back, Andrea was gone. A fear went through my body that I was not familiar with but I soon calmed down and thought it out; she was still on the ship but where? I immediately got another elevator car and went to the LIDO deck on the 9th level. She was nowhere to be found. I then went back to the cabin to tell Nickie that I had lost our granddaughter. She got dressed and left the cabin to search for her but soon realized that someone should be in the cabin so that if anyone called, someone would be there to answer. She paced the floor and prayed and about 5 minutes later the phone rang. Andrea had gone 2 floors up and spotted a Carnival worker to tell her story to: "My PaPa and I were going to breakfast and he was talking to a man and missed the elevator. She told them who she was and that her grandparents' names were Jerry and Nicole Bishop. Notice, she used Nickie's Christian name and not her nickname. They called the purser's office, got our cabin number and called to advise us that Andrea was waiting there for us. Oh by the way, she told them she was hungry too. Nickie asked her if she was upset when she noticed that her PaPa didn't get on the elevator with her and she said : "NO, I just found someone to help me, told them your name and they called you."

You will recall, I talked of losing $800K with a financial planner sometime back and even though it did change our standard of living, I will tell you without hesitation, I am truly blessed. I have something more important than money. I have a little girl that looks up to me and tells me she loves me at least 4 or 5 times a day.

Society calls this child "SPECIAL NEEDS". I agree SHE is a SPECIAL child. She is my granddaughter and she is very SPECIAL and very NORMAL by my standards.

If I could be allowed just one wish from Heaven, it would be that her mother JoAnn, our daughter, could see her just once as she is now. I am so proud of all she has accomplished in her short life. My day begins each and every morning when

I go into her room and there she is lying on her stomach with her arm around Snowflake, the stuffed cat her Great grandmother gave her. I pat her little bottom and she turns over and gives me the most beautiful smile I will see that day. What a wonderful life I have.

We read in the Bible that when God shuts one door, He opens another. Our daughter JoAnn was taken away prematurely at the age of 44 and in turn Andrea, a four-year-old sweet little girl, was given to us to love. One doesn't replace the other but it sure helped us cope with our loss.

I ask only one thing in return for writing this book. Don't feel sorry for me because I have a child with Down Syndrome to raise. Praise GOD on my behalf because I am one of only a few to be so blessed with such a **"GIFT FROM GOD"**!

The Bishop/Basler Family
PaPa, Andrea & Mommy

In memory of JoAnn

December 15th 1960 - June 25th 2005

Papa's Favorite Photos

Andrea 3 years old

Jerry Bishop

Oh that look!

Flower girl at friends' wedding

A Gift from GOD

Andrea 9 years old

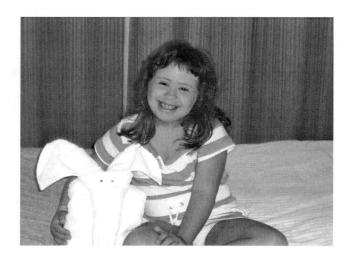

Andrea on cruise in 2010

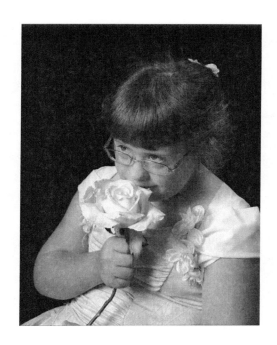

Dance recital 2011

We three

A Gift from GOD

Dance recital 2012